Crush Your Military Transition

Jeffrey Phillipy

ISBN-10: 0-9864228-0-0
ISBN-13: 978-0-9864228-0-5

Dedication

To my loving family,

Amy, Sophia, and Jaxon,

and

everyone who has served or is serving in the

United States military.

Contents

Acknowledgments

I want to thank my family and friends for listening to me talk nonstop about the topic of this book. I specifically want to mention Jeff Majer. I also need to thank those who have helped me understand what issues transitioning service members and veterans are challenged with. Brian Parrish and Christopher Gambill provided great wisdom and knowledge.

I'd like to give a special thank you to my team. Without them this would not have happened.

Editing: Joni Wilson www.elance.com/s/jmzwilson

Cover Design: Kirsten Moore www.behance.net/KMoore.

Introduction

Are you thinking about leaving the military? Deciding what civilian jobs you are qualified for? You chose the right book. The process I cover is geared toward military personnel, but it can also be helpful to civilians. No matter who you are, I can guide you through the process and help you *Crush Your Military Transition.*

I asked myself why veterans struggle after they exit the military. Many times I find it is due to lack of preparation. Studies have shown that more than half of the veterans who leave the military either don't know what they want to do or want time to decompress before beginning a civilian career. In the current job market, there is no time for decompressing.

You are not going to be one of those people. Throughout this book there are transition exercises that are going to build your confidence to make you successful. If you don't know what you want to do, I will help you discover what careers you are best suited for and help you find a new occupation.

What I want you to know from the beginning is that you are not alone. Millions of veterans have been where you are right now and have felt what you are feeling. Fear of finding your first civilian job, translating your military skills to civilian skills, lack of education or certifications, not relating to non-veteran civilians, and readjusting to a civilian social life are just some of the challenges you will work through. I will show you how to be successful by creating a personal timeline and setting goals.

One thing that bothers me is that veterans usually have to hide the fact they are considering leaving the military. I've seen many instances where leaders find out that veterans are actively preparing to leave the service, and the leaders look at the veterans as if they are quitters. I have heard the closed-door discussions where people get rated lower on their performance evaluations, not because they aren't performing, but because they are exiting the service. That just doesn't seem right to me.

When conducting their civilian job search, veterans use those evaluations to validate their skills and abilities. If you're in that situation, this book provides a great solution. You can plan your transition and not have to make appointments. You will end up with a better result than if you only use military-sponsored services.

Ideally you are, at a minimum, 24–36 months away from your transition date. If you are closer, you can accelerate this plan. No worries, I've got you covered. You will be successful. The simple fact that you bought this book tells me you are ready to put in the work needed to earn your success. I am going to give you a complete mental makeover to prepare you to trade in your military uniform for civilian clothes. It doesn't matter if you want to be a plumber or a banker; this process is one-size-fits-all. The key is to trust the process, roll with the punches, and do not quit.

I'm not here to write a 500-page book full of filler. This is a no-bullshit, how-to guide for you to take action toward achieving your goals. If you were looking for the same old guide (like you get in the Transition Assistance Programs designed by the military) you have the wrong book. Those books are for people who just want to get by. They are not crushing anything. They might do ok, get a decent job, and live a good life. Those other courses will not teach you how to take control of your life. I'm giving you the tools to get started doing what you truly want to do—live how you want to live. Are you ready to define your new life and begin to control your own destiny?

Let's Start Crushing It

You're about to go through a massive change in your life. To make things worse, with the military downsizing, it might not be by choice. However, whether you are retiring, medically discharged, or "downsized," today is the last day you are allowed to let your fear stop you from preparing for your transition. You don't have time for that. Your biggest enemy will be you during this critical time in your life.

Every day you're going to know that you made progress, and you will continue to grow the confidence necessary to *Crush Your Military Transition*. Attitude can get you past anything, and the resiliency you built during your time serving your country is going to push you through to the end. The power of the mind is amazing. You need to know that once you believe in yourself, you achieve more than you ever thought possible.

Start this process by downloading the transition management worksheet at crushyourtransition.com (you can print the form or use it electronically). Complete it as you work through the assessment portion of this book. That will help you keep all the information you need in one place. Then you can work through the exercises without having to track down additional information.

Pre-Reading Assignment

Before you begin, print the Pre-Reading Assignment (below or download at crushyourtransition.com) to begin your journey. Yes, I said "assignment." I told you that you have to do some hard work for your transition to be successful. It is important to use terminology that reflects the requirement for the work to be completed.

I don't want you to even start reading the first page being unprepared. You will gain more knowledge by reading with a purpose and knowing what result you are working toward. This is part of making you more efficient. One idea I learned in the military was to go slowly at first, to go fast later. Looking back, I wish I would have used this before I began preparing for my transition.

Using the worksheet prior to reading Chapter 2 on skills assessment will help you know what your initial goals are. This is important because I first want you to have what you think you want. Then you can compare it to what you decide you want after you get through the book. That way you can see how well you thought you knew yourself and what you learned along the way.

If you don't want to print the Pre-Reading Assignment now or you don't have a printer available, pull out a blank piece of paper. I'm not going to give you an excuse to not complete this. You can even write your answers in the book. I made sure to leave some room for you to scribble.

1. What are your occupations of interest?

2. What are your personal work values and ethics?

3. What are your skills and special qualifications?

4. What is your desired quality of life?

5. What are your geographic areas of interest?

1 Preparing for Change

"If you do what you've always done, you'll get what you've always gotten."
—Anthony Robbins

It's Time for Something Different

I love this Tony Robbins quote, because it relates directly to your transition. If you think of yourself the same way you have for the past 10–20 years, you're going to see yourself the same way you always have. The first thing you need to understand is that you are not going to be in the military anymore. I know you know that, but do you understand what that means? I want you to say it out loud and listen to yourself. When you hear it, does it sound different?

Many people have a hard time with the beginning of their transition, because they have been identifying themselves as soldiers, marines, airmen, and sailors for so long. It will take a lot of work to get past that mentality. We will go through some branding exercises to get you through it and then you can see yourself in a different light.

I am going to teach you to look deeper inside yourself than you ever have before. I want to help unlock your maximum potential. This process will force you to leave your comfort zone to realize what you are truly capable of.

I'll tell you when to use the military-sponsored Transition Assistance Program (TAP) closer to the time that you plan to leave. It is good, but only to a point. Whether you have completed 3 years or 20 years of service, you need to take advantage of all available resources to prepare for your transition. Many people take the process too lightly. The output from the process is your life. I think that is a really important result to focus on. Transition programs have good information about resources, but they don't have time to focus directly on you. My process will teach you to use the tools available and prepare yourself for success.

When you leave the military, it's up to you to be concerned about your civilian transition. Your unit has missions and personnel issues to tend to. It is ready to focus on the personnel remaining in the military. Budget cuts are going to continue well into the future and threats are emerging around the globe. I just don't see the transition programs improving anytime soon, and I wouldn't bet my livelihood on someone else doing the work for me.

Most job fairs sponsored by the military offer general positions that only appeal to a small percentage of transitioning personnel. The resume classes available are the basic "copy and paste from other resume formats" and "check the block" type of classes we are all use to. Free civilian certification programs worth completing will never be heard of. I find that completely unacceptable.

The military-sponsored books are geared toward the lowest common denominator. They are basically reference books filled with external sources and organizations that lead you in a million directions leaving you to figure everything out on your own. I do not consider any of this overly helpful to the transitioning veteran.

Mentality

Most of you have served your country during a time of war. You know what it is like to be in bad places and go through hard times. You have the resiliency, determination, and desire to succeed. If you are like me, the only thing you need to succeed is a little confidence in your abilities. I felt the need to take a chance, and the action I took was creating this book, which was the boost of confidence I needed to get this program up and running.

Striving to be who you want to be is the only way you will ever reach your goal. Wishing, hoping, and talking about what you want to do will get you right where you are right now. A lot of people talk about doing things. This is one reason you want to plan your transition ahead of time. You need to get involved in the field you want to work in before you leave the military. We will dive further into this, but if you are this far into the book, you are ready to make the change and improve your life.

Goals, Timelines, and Deadlines

Studies average that 95 percent of people are lying to themselves. By that I mean they talk about goals they would like to have happen. The thing is stuff doesn't just happen; you have to put in the work. Three years ago I lost 55 pounds in 12 weeks. It was the most structured activity I've done, outside of work. I even scheduled my meals and had daily micro goals to guarantee daily improvement.

What happened to the other 5 percent, who didn't lie to themselves? They included deadlines and milestones along with their plans. New Year's resolutions are a joke. I think we can all admit that. The 5 percent of people who were dedicated and planned the timeline for their goals made it through the journey. Remember, deadlines turn dreams into goals.

I want to lose some weight. I want to work out more. Those sound kind of vague. What do you really want to accomplish? I want to lose 20 pounds. This person is more specific and will have a better chance of being successful. I am going to lose 20 pounds by July and will track my progress weekly. This person has a plan and will have the best chance to be part of the proud 5 percent.

To achieve a goal, you need a written plan with a method of daily tracking or some measurement of progress. The last example (of a person who wants to lose weight) has made a commitment and believes it can be achieved. They will most likely have a workout plan to hold themselves accountable. They will make deadlines along the way in order to stay on track to meet the goal.

The deadlines and milestones are what will get you to your goal. This is the way you should commit to your transition. Write your plan with milestones you want to meet along the way. You need to specify that you want to research your ideal positions by X date and begin translating your skills by X date and map out your entire transition.

This is why transitions take time. You have to put in work to be successful. Just like there is no miracle weight loss pill, no training class is going to give you the magic potion to find success. It just takes practice, and you have to work at it to keep improving.

Where to Begin

I want you to begin at the end. Think about where you want to be at the end of your transition. Where do you want to live? What do you want to be doing? What does your family situation look like? Seriously, close your eyes and visualize your future. We are beginning your journey right now.

These can be broadly written statements. At this point you are putting general goals on paper and will narrow them down later. Go all the way to think about how healthy you want to be. Do you want more education? Take your time to think about it.

This will help you visualize what you want. As you take your time to go through this, you need to decide if all your goals are achievable. You need to believe that each goal is honestly achievable within a five-year timeline. You might want to beat athlete LeBron James in a game of one-on-one basketball, but is that achievable? You can extend your goals later, but keep it within a five-year timeline right now.

You can use any format you want to. It needs to be comfortable for you to use, because this will be your road map to your future. You will keep it as a working document. I have some templates on the website (crushyourtransition.com) in different formats. Download one or create your own. I just want you to use it.

Let me give you some of my broad goals.

1. $150K in the bank for my emergency fund.

2. I need to be involved in the community.

3. Maintain an active network of people I actually know.

4. Make sure my family is involved in the transition process.

5. Be my own boss or have a family business.

6. Travel the world and enjoy different cultures.

This is a good place to begin. Construct a broad base to build from. Don't lock yourself into any specific career field, because you haven't yet arrived at that step. You will get to that when you assess your strengths and weaknesses.

Where Do I Go from Here

To properly plan your goals, you need to look at how much time you have before your proposed transition date. For our purposes in this book, we will say you have two years. Now we can lay out the short-, medium-, and long-term goals.

Let's set your short-term timeline for one year. This will give you the time you need to get some small victories and build some momentum. Your first short-term goal might be to learn what is required to have a successful transition. You are doing that right now. Remember what I said before. You need to first start slowly to go fast later. You are going to do your preparation and not waste time building resumes and other products before you know what you are qualified to do and how to show you are qualified.

Remember, make your short-term goals meaningful and achievable. One method to make these goals more achievable is to break down your short-term goals into smaller micro goals. Micro goals are monthly tasks that will build up to completing your short-term goals on time. By breaking these down into smaller increments, you are laying out the action plan that will validate your short-term timeline.

This will also help you make daily progress. With monthly milestones, you will be more likely to avoid procrastination. If you have a goal for the year, you could easily not begin working toward your goal until the nine-month mark. As a matter of fact, if you know you are a procrastinator, I would advise you to make weekly goals. It is all about having the forcing function to get you to make daily progress on your transition. If you spend 20 minutes a day, I almost guarantee that you will reach your short-term goal early.

After one year you will be ready to begin chipping away at medium-range goals. Your medium-range goal can also be a year. This will take you up to your transition date. These goals will consist of building your network and preparing for the culture change you are about to experience. You will do this by planning conferences and other events you will attend dealing with your industry. You will also want to begin a blog or create some type of Web content to present yourself as an authority in your industry.

Here is a secret for you. If you have a blog or a podcast, you can request a press pass to gain access to events. Use that as an additional tool to get meaningful time with people. Ask for interviews with influencers in the industry and post them on your blog. Then email the person and let him or her know where it is posted. This will keep you higher on the radar.

You are doing this to build your network before you want a job. Too many people are "networking" and immediately asking for a job. You will set yourself apart by really just helping people with what they need. Then, after building these relationships, you could literally have people asking you when you are available rather than the other way around.

Finally, your long-term goals will extend three to five years past your retirement from the military. This way you are already working on your larger goals as you are leaving the service. Your long-term goals are going to help you decide which companies you want to interview with.

For extra credit you can move your phases as you complete them. For example, after the first year you might shift your medium-range goals to short-term goals on your plan. Then the long-term becomes medium. By doing this you will stay motivated to keep improving and making progress.

Embrace Your Passion

"Take a chance, Columbus did."
—Joey Diaz

During your transition you are going to have to make many decisions about your career choices. That is why I asked to really think about what you wanted to do. Some people are looking for big money, while others are searching for the best location. Keep in mind that this is your chance to decide what would make you happy.

Some people don't know what type of career they want. The people in this group have to go out and follow their curiosity to find what they are truly interested in. When you change careers, you can't focus solely on money. Happiness is a big part of life. Busy people who work 17 hours a day and feel super-important can be miserable and have three heart attacks by the time they are 60. In contrast, photographers who get to enjoy nature and peace in the world might only make enough money to live a modest life, but they are truly enjoying work and life.

Don't set limits on yourself when you are transitioning. You shouldn't go find a job that you think you have to go after because it aligns with the career field you are currently in. This is your chance to start fresh. If this sounds intriguing the chapter on entrepreneurship might be for you. So many people are unsatisfied with their careers, but do not have the courage to make a change in their lives. This is your opportunity to take control of your life and do what you want to do.

If you are thinking about embracing your passion, here are some thoughts on how to start out.

What are you good at?

What makes you lose your sense of time when you are involved in it?

What talents do you have that you could monetize?

Are you willing to take a chance?

Don't make this decision on your own. If you have family, discuss it with them. Consider the financial impacts and work that into your planning. You should also connect with some people who are involved in the industry and get their point of view on what is involved in becoming successful. You can request an informational interview and meet with people and discuss the industry. Do not ask for a job, this request is only for information.

It is also important to realize that when you strive to embrace your passion during a career change, you will most likely experience failure on some level. Don't let that discourage you. Embracing the early failure will only help you hone your skills and abilities to make you more successful. When you can work in a career you truly love, you aren't really working. The earlier you begin your transition, the better prepared you will be if you take this route. As you move into the assessment phase you will see what your strengths are and discover what you are best suited for. Don't rule out careers you actually want to get involved with.

Realize Your True Value

Self-awareness is having a clear perception of your strengths, weaknesses, thoughts, beliefs, motivations, and emotions. You need to understand yourself before you can go through the rest of this process. I know the military tells us we need to know ourselves to be leaders, but many service members do not truly know who they really are deep inside.

This issue isn't just a military problem. People in general have a denial about their true selves. We spend so much time identifying ourselves by what we do, what we like, and others around us, but seldom do we really identify with who we really are. Year after year we identify ourselves by our occupation or material possessions. That stops now.

Extremely successful people have one thing in common. They are happy, confident, and willing to embrace themselves. People who are happy with who they are don't waste time worrying about what people think about them and their ideas. This gives them a greater ability to be creative and focus on their goals.

Self-awareness isn't the magic answer to your transition, but it is the important first step that most people overlook. I would say that the average service member looks at the goal and then plans and moves out to execute. You have to evaluate your two most important resources to complete your transition. You and time. Understand yourself and the amount of time you have until you begin a new chapter in your life.

To get started, you have to get your mind wrapped around these two facts.

You do have value.

You are worth achieving success.

These ideas might not seem like a big deal. The truth is, we all greatly undervalue ourselves when we begin the transition to civilian life. I was also guilty of this. I thought I knew the limits of the value I could offer a company. After some further evaluation, I was disgustingly undervaluing myself. Even as I write this, I have to resist the urge to stop. I have to convince myself with every word and sentence that I am adding value to your life by sharing this book and this process with you. I could just keep it to myself, but I guarantee that you will get a huge return on your investment from the money you spent.

Many times when people look at themselves, they compare what they see to others. Or they look at the failures they had and decrease the value they bring to the world. You have to look deep inside to do this. You make your own reality in the world. What people do not understand is that we have the ability to control our lives and how others see us. A lot of the doubt and anxiety that we have comes from our own bullshit.

There is so much that we take for granted that other people value. If we could know the gifts we give to others on a daily basis, we would know the true value we bring to them. If you are reading this book, you clearly want to improve.

Once you gain a deeper understanding of yourself and your abilities, your self-confidence will grow exponentially. Your confidence will take you far. I want you to learn the basic value you bring to the world daily, because you are building a campaign to sell yourself during your transition. It doesn't matter if you are having a yard sale or you are in a million-dollar business deal, if you are not confident, you will not close the deal. You need to close this deal, and the future you want is going to take effort to achieve. We begin that work right here.

Value Exercise

Go to work and ask some people you deal with on a regular basis what value you bring to their lives. I guarantee that you will be surprised at what you hear. Write down what they tell you and when you begin looking at your strengths and weaknesses, you can reflect on the comments you received. You can then apply those comments to your skills translation. In turn, this will strengthen pitches to employers in your resume and interview answers.

What's Your Story?

I had to change my story to be successful. I see you shaking your head trying to figure out what I mean. We are full of stories. We tell ourselves what we can and can't do. I will get deeper into this when I discuss beating your fear. However, you can't find your passion in life until you identify your self-limiting stories.

These are the stories we tell ourselves that begin with, "I can't do that" or "I'm not good enough for that." You have to get past this and create new stories full of confidence and visions of you completing your goals and dreams. These are your stories that you are creating to keep you from "failing" when you are too afraid to try. Everyone who tries is going to know failure; it's what you do with the failure that will define you. Remember what hockey legend Wayne Gretzky said, "You will miss 100 percent of the shots you don't take."

Exercise 1: Evaluating Your Military Experience

There are most likely things you loved about being in the military and others that you are glad you never have to do again. As you go through the following topics, you can choose whether you would keep it or toss it. Some topics you might want to choose both, but go with your gut on this. You can print additional forms online in the free download section.

Topic	Keep It	Toss It
Tasks/Responsibilities		
Utilization of Skills		
People		
Values		
Work Environment		
Other		

Case Study 1: Slow and Steady Success

Brian was an Army military police officer for five years and earned the rank of sergeant. After leaving the service he knew he wanted to do something else, he just wasn't sure what he wanted to do. In the meantime he used his military experience to obtain a good paying security position in Washington DC.

After looking at his options, he decided to choose something different from the work he had been doing for the past couple of years. Brian returned to school and received his bachelor's degree in computer networking. He worked in the computer-networking field for nearly a decade earning his master of business administration (MBA) and doctoral (PhD) degrees. Growing tired of the managing day-to-day networking issues, he left to pursue a teaching career at a local university.

Brian always had an entrepreneurial drive and decided he was comfortable enough to give it a try. He obtained the proper permits and started a home-based gun dealership. He was working fulltime teaching during the day, and working nights and weekends on his side venture. In three years he was selling $1,000–$2,000 per month in merchandise from his home.

His growing business was considered successful for a home-based gun dealer, but Brian knew he wanted more. He saw the effort that he put in his business as an investment to maintain his lifestyle after he finished teaching. He began discussions with a friend who had a small local gun dealership. Brian and his new partner brought in one financial backer and opened a new gun store in a high-traffic shopping center.

With the move, Brian's monthly sales skyrocketed to an average of $80,000–$100,000 per month. Through his persistent struggle to succeed, he slowly grew professionally and was able to make his entrepreneurial dream come true. Currently he is planning to expand the business to a second retail location and a move into manufacturing custom weapons to bid on contracts from local law enforcement.

A Closer Look

Diving deeper into this story, we can learn some lessons from Brian. First, unlike many veterans, he didn't look at what he was trained to do. He sought out what he was interested in. Taking advantage of his G.I. Bill, he returned to school to allow him to make his transition into a new career field.

Prior to his exit from the military, he made sure his finances were on track and he started his new journey debt free. He found another veteran also leaving the service at the same time. That veteran just happened to be me. We split the bills, stayed home a lot, and poured our energy into going to school and working extra hours to pay for it. When you have a goal, you have to sacrifice to make it a reality.

Throughout the years he never allowed himself to maintain a level of comfort. He was always striving for the next level and making sure his family had a higher level of security. I truly believe that once you feel comfortable, you stop improving. Success requires you to keep moving out of your comfort zone.

2 Skills Assessment

There are many tasks that military personnel perform on a regular basis, which are never considered as areas of expertise. Translating your military skills into a language a civilian hiring manager will understand isn't an easy process. This section of chapter 2 will walk you through in stages to make the process less complicated and intimidating.

First, let me give you an example of some of the skills you might overlook. This will give you a frame of reference before you begin your translation process. How often have you had to plan and execute an operation with multiple phases? Probably more times than you can even remember. Let's begin by taking a closer look at how you can easily translate your military experience into a project management certification.

Project Management

When you translate your military service, most senior noncommissioned officers and officers have the required 4,500 hours to qualify for the Project Management Professional (PMP) exam. Along with that you can receive the 35 hours of required training free from two different sources if you are still in the military. The first source is through the Skillsoft training online. The PMP course is certified to meet the requirements for the Project Management Institute (PMI) testing. You do have to request your certificates to prove your training.

The second source is through the Syracuse University Veterans Career Transition Program (VCTP). The program is paid for by JPMorgan Chase. You have access to a student advisor and have to pass the practice exam twice with an 80 percent score before taking the PMP exam. The VCTP covers your exam fees; the Skillsoft option does not. If you want pay to receive training on your own, it would cost you between $100–$1,000 depending on the source and quality of the training.

The main areas of responsibility for a project manager are managing the resources, scope, and schedule of projects. **Resources** include assigning people and equipment to a project. **Scope** includes adding and removing tasks and assignment in the project. **Schedule** includes speeding up or extending the project timeline.

You have performed all those requirements during your career in the military. You just have to list your deployments, field training, exercises, range operations, and functions you planned and break down the hours. I have the templates on crushyourtransition.com to get you the rest of the way.

Safety

Another area where you add more value to a company is your background in safety. You couldn't walk three feet in the military without thinking about safety. Everything you did, from physical training to weapons qualification, required you to complete a risk assessment and find mitigation strategies for the risks you identified. Many times these assessments were most likely three to five pages long.

Let's look at some of the tasks I'm talking about to get you started.

Range Operations: planning, ammunition forecasting and management, personnel management, resource forecasting and management, safety, transportation management and range operations.

Functions: Planning, menu and food services, seating and timeline management, VIP considerations, budget and sales, promotion. It takes a lot of time management and organizational skills to create a successful event. Whether it is a reception or a military ball, you will most likely have a budget of several thousand dollars to tens of thousands of dollars. You also managed a team of people who were responsible for different parts of the function, and you separated those people into functional teams to more easily manage a sizable operation.

Safety: Operational, personal, hazardous material, and workplace safety are all functions most military personnel have all been responsible for. Most personnel have more experience in safety considerations than 90 percent of civilians performing the same functions. Safety includes your experience with risk management. In the military, risk management is used daily in everything from physical training to the heat index for work details. The ability to take factors that pose a risk and identify methods of mitigation is also beyond what most civilians can comprehend. Again, this is something you can use to your advantage in finding a civilian career.

The three subjects listed above are used in the example skills translator, which can be downloaded for you to use on crushyourtransition.com. This will give you a better idea of what you need to extract from your records to make sure none of your skills are overlooked.

In the following section we will work on breaking down your skills into three categories: Transferable skills, technical skills, and Personal traits. This an important step, because the deeper you dissect your military experience you will be able to translate more of your skills.

Transferable Skills

Transferable skills are general skills that can be used in a variety of careers. These can come from any activity in which you have participated: parenting, education, hobbies, sports or volunteering. There is a misconception that transferable skills need to come from your work experience and that just isn't true.

Consider the following four questions when deciding your skills.

1. **Value** = What value do you add to the position/company?

2. **Intelligence** = How intellectually prepared are you to take on the responsibility?

3. **Social / Networking** = How connected are you in the industry? What potential connections can you add?

4. **Performance** = To what extent can you improve the current environment and perform the required tasks?

The following is a list of often overlooked transferable skills.

- Communication
- Motivation/Initiative
- Teamwork
- Leadership
- Interpersonal
- Flexibility/Adaptability
- Technical
- Honesty/Integrity
- Work Ethic
- Analytical/Problem Solving

Use the list of skills below to determine your transferable skills proficiency. Check all the skills you think you are proficient in. Then circle the five skills you feel are your strongest. Underline the five skills you enjoy the most. Finally, put an X next to the five skills you want to improve. These checks can be the same or different skills.

This list is not all inclusive. If you think of any additional skills, be sure to add them on a separate sheet of paper. Later we will focus your stronger skills toward your desired career field and work to qualify and quantify them for your resume.

____Advising	____Explaining	____Observing
____Analyzing	____Expressing	____Operating
____Anticipating	____Formulating	____Persuading
____Assembling	____Fundraising	____Planning
____Assessing	____Gathering	____Predicting
____Auditing	____Generating	____Processing
____Budgeting	____Group Facilitating	____Programming
____Classifying	____Implementing	____Promoting
____Coaching	____Influencing	____Protecting
____Collecting	____Initiating	____Purchasing
____Conceptualizing	____Inspecting	____Questioning
____Controlling	____Inspiring	____Reading
____Coordinating	____Instructing	____Recording
____Corresponding	____Integrating	____Recruiting
____Creating	____Interpreting	____Rehabilitating
____Dealing with Pressure	____Interviewing	____Repairing
____Deciding	____Investigating	____Researching
____Delegating	____Leading	____Selling
____Displaying	____Listening	____Speaking
____Distributing	____Locating	____Supervising
____Editing	____Managing	____Teaching
____Entertaining	____Mediating	____Understanding
____Estimating	____Monitoring	____Verbalizing
____Examining	____Motivating	____Visualizing
____Exhibiting	____Negotiating	____Writing

Technical Skills

Technical skills are the knowledge and capabilities to perform specialized tasks. These skills are gained through education training, work experience, and life experience. These skills include using Microsoft Office, maintaining technical reports, and using computer languages.

List the top five technical skills you would like to use in your next position.

1.

2.

3.

4.

5.

List the top five technical skills you want to develop for your next position.

1.

2.

3.

4.

5.

Personal Traits

Personal traits are distinguishing qualities that are at the center of an individual's character. They are your habitual patterns of behavior, temperament and emotion. These are initially learned during your childhood years and later in life through training courses for self-improvement.

To evaluate yourself, read each trait below and check the skills that describe you. To further analyze your skills, underline the five skills that most describe you. Circle the five skills you want to develop. Print some extra pages and ask others to complete what they think your top five skills are. Compare your results with what others say.

____Accurate	____Disciplined	____Intuitive
____Active	____Discreet	____Inventive
____Adaptable	____Dynamic	____Knowledgeable
____Adventurous	____Eager	____Logical
____Aggressive	____Efficient	____Loyal
____Ambitious	____Emotional	____Mature
____Anticipative	____Energetic	____Meticulous
____Artistic	____Enthusiastic	____Modest
____Attractive	____Firm	____Objective
____Balanced	____Flexible	____Optimistic
____Broadminded	____Friendly	____Organized
____Captivating	____Generous	____Original
____Charismatic	____Gentle	____Outgoing
____Charming	____Genuine	____Passionate
____Cheerful	____Hardworking	____Rational
____Clever	____Helpful	____Realistic
____Competent	____Honest	____Reflective
____Competitive	____Honorable	____Resourceful
____Confident	____Humble	____Responsible
____Conservative	____Humorous	____Self-confident
____Cooperative	____Idealistic	____Self-controlled
____Courageous	____Imaginative	____Sensible
____Curious	____Independent	____Sensitive
____Deliberate	____Industrious	____Steadfast
____Diplomatic	____Intelligent	____Well-Rounded

Strengths

You have just completed the first big step to *Crush Your Military Transition.* You put in the work to carefully assess yourself. Right now you should have a lengthy list of what your strengths are. If you don't think you captured everything, feel free to do this again and explore yourself further. Be honest with yourself. The more honest you are now, the more efficient your job search will be.

This can be a hard moment. You might be realizing that you aren't where you need to be for the civilian career that you want. You might be lacking some work experience or training. This isn't the end of the world, and it is definitely not time to forget your goal.

You should be starting to realize the importance of working on your transition planning as early as possible. I would do this at least three years before you think about leaving the service. You will know exactly where you stand and have time to create an action plan with enough time to improve your situation before you prepare to exit the military.

I have talked to veterans who have applied for more than 500 jobs and went to 75 interviews and still didn't get a job offer. My goal is to have you understand the reality you are facing. Being a veteran isn't going to guarantee you a good job. Understanding this will save you a lot of frustration during your transition. Every month you don't have a civilian job, you are losing money, so it makes sense to plan for maximum efficiency.

Weaknesses

You also have to focus on the weaknesses in your skill set. There are many ways to figure out what you need to add to your skill set to make yourself competitive for your dream position. Some of the weaknesses I believe many veterans will have include sales, marketing, and the understanding of the importance of revenue against the bottom line.

For veterans, the military is more about staying within budget and mission accomplishment. This could be one area where you might need to do some classroom or self-study training to teach yourself to speak intelligently on these specific subjects during an interview.

Some of you might be wondering how to assess what skills you need to improve. I think the best way is to look at job descriptions in the areas you are interested in. Compare the requirements that employers are asking for with your skill sets. If there are skills that you are expected to know about, make a list of the key weaknesses you need to improve. Prioritize those tasks and research the best ways to gain more knowledge about those topics.

Pay close attention to the specific wording in the job listings. For example, there are a lot of listings in the area of logistics that desire managers with a knowledge of the principles of Six Sigma. Knowledge of the principles is a lot different than having a certification. A certification, depending on where you get the training and testing, can be pricey. You could buy a book for $80 and buckle down and learn the key principles through self-study. Then you will be able to discuss the principles during an interview.

Initially, the applicant with the certification might look better on paper. However, if the applicant who bought the book and studied was able to discuss the principles and how to implement them in the company better than the person with the certification, he can earn the position. Just having a certification isn't worth the money, if you can't discuss the subject and teach others about the topic.

Optimize Your Job Campaign

I saw the term "job campaign" on the Internet, and it really just stuck in my head. I'm all about being in the right mentality when you want to achieve your goal. The word "campaign" is a better choice for the way I teach people to go into the mental preparation phase of their transition from the military.

One of the main issues I run into is the transitioning service members who think they should enter civilian employment at the same level and pay as when they left the military. Just because you were at a certain level in the military doesn't mean you will start at the same level as a civilian. Most veterans, especially if they don't prepare early, are forced to take a step back when they enter the civilian market.

The reason is not because they are lacking the capability to be successful in a higher position. It is because they don't know the new civilian jargon for that industry along with the new norms and values. These people have to work their way up and learn the system to develop into more effective leaders for the organization. This is why I tell veterans to attend conferences and events in your industry. You can learn about the industry and possibly talk your way into a better position in your interview.

One way to avoid starting at the bottom and save a lot of time is to optimize your job campaign by properly evaluating your skills from the start. Normally when we assess our strengths and weaknesses, we do it in a general sense and just look at what we do well and what we need to improve. If you are truly assessing yourself, you have to measure it against something. What is better to measure it against than the position you want to apply for at the company you want to work for? Let's get in the trenches and crush this assessment.

To begin, list your top five job positions that you want to apply for and the top five companies you want to interview with. Do a job search; find job postings that match with your list and print them.

Highlight all the required skills in the postings and input them on the form shown here. If there are duplicate skills, you only need them listed once. In the first column. list the required skills from the positions that you highlighted. In the second column, write yes or no if you have the skill or not. In the third column, write if you have any experience close to the skills you marked "no." For example, if the listing wants five years of experience and you have three years, write that in the third column.

Desired Skills	Yes or No	My Skills

This exercise will show you two things. First, you will better understand what skills the employers in your desired industry expect potential employees to have. Second, you will see if you are underqualified for the types of positions you are looking to be employed in or if you are underachieving and maybe need to look at a higher level position that will better fit your skill set and increase your pay.

Either way, this will optimize the efficiency in your job campaign by narrowing your focus before you get started, which will allow you to direct your efforts to the top jobs that match your skills and abilities. Your chances to land the position you want will increase greatly by selecting your target with full self-awareness, saving you both time and energy.

Service members should always ensure they remain relevant in their civilian equivalent. This would prevent them from trying to gain the necessary knowledge and transition at the same time.

With the military in a drawdown period, more people are being medically discharged and passed over for promotions. Nothing is guaranteed anymore. Skip an episode of your favorite TV show and begin your preparation by keeping your assessments and your résumé up to date. You can spend a couple of hours a month and stay relevant in your industry. It will pay huge dividends by reducing stress when you do decide to begin your transition.

Resources

O*NET Online (www.onetonline.org) is a great resource to assist you in translating your skills to make them easily understood. The site allows you to search for your service specific job title and assists in the translation of tasks, skills and other variables. Below is an example of the skills for an 11B infantryman in the Army. They sound like marketable skills to me. Now all you have to do is quantify them to match your performance. Half the work is done for you. The points even begin with your action verbs.

If you were an infantryman and worked in the orderly room or in the supply room, look up those job titles and mix in the skills that fit. Don't limit yourself. Any cross-functional work you performed should be used when you translate your skills.

➤ Prepare training budget for department or organization.

➤ Evaluate instructor performance and the effectiveness of training programs, providing recommendations for improvement.

➤ Analyze training needs to develop new training programs or modify and improve existing programs.

➤ Conduct or arrange for ongoing technical training and personal development classes for staff members.

➤ Plan, develop and provide training and staff development programs, using knowledge of the effectiveness of methods, such as classroom training, demonstrations, on-the-job training, meetings, conferences and workshops.

➤ Conduct orientation sessions and arrange on-the-job training for new hires.

➤ Confer with management and conduct surveys to identify training needs based on projected production processes, changes and other factors.

➤ Train instructors and supervisors in techniques and skills for training and dealing with employees.

➤ Develop and organize training manuals, multimedia visual aids and other educational materials.

➤ Develop testing and evaluation procedures.

When you look at the skills listed above and compare them to the skills most requested by employers, you can make matches to nearly everything employers want.

➤ Leadership

➤ Analysis

➤ Human Resources

➤ Training

➤ Recruiting

➢ Problem Solving

➢ Networking

➢ Presentations

➢ Access

➢ Finance

When you really look at it, I think service members think too technical about their skills. When you look at your military service, look at what tasks and functions you performed during your service. Your biggest mistake would be limiting yourself to just your job title.

I said it already but I can't stress it enough. It's about the tasks and skills you performed. You conducted inventories, signed for equipment, took care of personnel issues, planned and executed countless missions, analyzed safety issues, and performed under pressure. Do not sell yourself short, translate your entire experience. This is why preparation is important. You most likely have forgotten more achievements than you can remember.

3 Rebranding

Reputation

What is your reputation? We are going to go through the process now to decide what your reputation is. What do other people say about you when you are not in the room? My guess is that you have some idea. To verify your thoughts, ask some people you know will be honest with you. Hopefully you won't be surprised, in a bad way.

Here are the real questions you want to ask the people you work with.

How do I make people feel?

What value do I add to people's lives personally or professionally?

What words do people use to describe me?

Once you understand how you are viewed by others, you can compare it to how you want to be seen. The amount of work will differ from person to person. The road to get from who you are to who you want to be doesn't have to be hard. Like everything in life, you just have to be willing to do the work.

Discussions throughout this book will constantly return to the subject of your reputation. Both online and off, how you are viewed will come into play. You are going to be everywhere—you will have a presence in your community, on social media, and anywhere else you can think of by the end of this process.

Rebranding Yourself

We briefly discussed the importance of your reputation and what your reputation really is. What I want you to understand is that you have the ability to create and control the narrative that you want the world to see. It doesn't matter if that is how the world has seen you up to this point. You can take control of your brand during your transition.

Your brand will help you reach the customers or employers you want to connect with. This **first step** in branding is defining who you are, where you want to go, and how you plan to get there. The **second step** is defining who you want to reach. Who is you desired customer or industry?

This process is called "defining your avatar." For example, my avatar for this book is a 42-year-old senior military leader, with a family, transitioning from the military. I'm going to name my avatar Stacy, because it could be a man or a woman. Stacy likes coffee and doesn't have a lot of time to take in information. Stacy needs valuable content and easily accessible resources that take about 30 minutes out of his/her day. The resources have to be easy for Stacy to take to work or retrieve remotely.

Stacy is educated with either a master's degree or is working toward one. Stacy is also competitive for a civilian job, but either doesn't believe it or just needs some direction to get going in the right direction. Stacy might need an additional skill or two and a better understanding of how to use social media to enhance a job search and networking.

That is the target person for this book. Although anyone can use the information, I am writing it with Stacy in mind. You can't please everyone so you have to choose your ideal target audience member and begin there.

Here are the key elements that your avatar should include to properly narrow it down to your ideal target audience.

Demographic—age, gender, geographic location

Lifestyle—employment, family, home, transportation

Personality—generous, determined, optimistic, pedantic

Interests—hobbies, sports, favorite travel destinations, reading matter, TV programs

Favorite things—three things they wouldn't be without right now

You can see why businesses use this approach to verify who their target audience really is. My target audience is a mid-career to retiree age male or female in a senior leadership role who is transitioning from the military.

I'm not saying that first-term soldiers can't benefit from the process in this book. I'm pointing out that I'm not directing it toward them. I believe that most people leaving the military (as an E-1 to E-5) can get a lot of benefit from the services offered through the Transition Assistance Program. If you look at my focus area, there is a lot more at stake for them by being more likely to have larger families and more invested in the military.

Below I'll walk you through what you need to accomplish to decide how to brand yourself. The *Crush Your Military Transition* Personal Brand worksheet is in the free download section on crushyourtransition.com, along with my Personal Brand worksheet to use as an example. I filled out my worksheet when I started my personal website and blog.

Personal Branding Exercise

Mission: This gives clarity to what you are about and how you want to live your life. Everyone needs to have a mission statement. If you are retiring, I'm sure you have worked on mission statements before.

Vision: This describes what you want to become

I will become a leader in my organization, helping transform it into an organization that respects all customers and employees, while at the same time being the best husband and father I can be.

Job Knowledge Strengths: The value you add to make you the person companies should want to hire.

Personal X Factor: What is one thing that makes you unique and different from others in your niche?

Personal Traits: What about your personality makes you special?

Education and Work Experience: This is self-explanatory.

Goals: How do your short-, medium-, and long-term goals line up with the brand you are showing the world? Is the current you in line with the vision of the future you?

My Adventure in Personal Branding

When I decided to begin my personal website I had no idea how I wanted to set it up. I did know what I wanted to do, but the issue was how to communicate it. I already showed you the branding format I used, but I will show you my actual worksheet that I developed. Feel free to compare it to my website at www.jphillipy.com and see if you think my worksheet matches my brand.

Jeffrey Phillipy Personal Brand

Mission: Improve the lives of transitioning military personnel and veterans through mentorship and personal interaction in my network

Vision: I want to be the leader in individual transition planning and mentoring for the military community.

Job Knowledge Strengths: Knowledge of the weaknesses in the current transition process, network of transitioning personnel, communication skills, preparation skills, defining the value of veterans, the ability to help others.

Personal X Factor: I am giving people the same process I used to plan my separation. I have researched and listened to experts in each field to develop the most complete separation plan of attack and how-to guide.

Personal Traits: I honestly care about the people I work with. A lot of people are just doing this for the money and not offering the measure of quality that I do. I hold the core military values close to my soul as I work with each individual I assist. I have relationships with civilian recruiters to get the names of the people I help out in the public to land them a job faster.

Education and Work Experience: Master's degree in logistics; 13 years of experience in mentoring and coaching; 2 years of assisting others in transition planning. Relevant knowledge of how to leverage social media use and personal branding to get right message to the public.

Goals

Short Term—Complete my book and begin podcast. Build my network to spread the word of my services. Begin by selling the book as a self-published ebook. Get professional photos taken to use on social media and websites to improve the image while I'm on leave.

Mid Term—Conduct a soft launch of the video courses to friends who are transitioning from the military to work out any bugs or add information I might have missed. Use those people to also spread the word about the upcoming course launch.

Long Term—Video course is launched and begin research on a second book. Reassess what to add to the program to begin more one-on-one mentoring services and an elite group for people ready to achieve a higher level of success. Have people who found success with the program on the podcast.

4 Social Media

Social Media Overview

Let's put the bottom line up front. In the current job market, you need to be on social media. It is only going to get more important as we move into the future. Paper résumés are still a requirement and will continue to be used, but you need to have an online presence. Your goal with social media is to extend the reach of your résumé. It enables you to extend your network and connect with people you wouldn't normally be able to meet.

The first thing you have to do is develop a strategy to maximize your efforts. How involved do you want to be? Are you comfortable with social media, or do you have to get some experience as you start your transition?

You need to be able to be seen on social media. Your first task is to Google yourself. Enter your name in an online search engine. Look at what information is listed about you on the first two pages of results. Is there anything you don't want a future employer to see? Is there nothing there about you? There might be people listed with the same name as you. Look at what is listed about them. The last thing you want is for a criminal with the same name as you to be listed and employers question if that is you. Your potential employment could end there.

I know you are saying it's not your fault. Yes, it is your fault. What did you do to make sure that you were controlling your Web presence? If your answer is nothing, then you deserve to not get the interview. Don't let the Internet control your future.

The only way to grab that control back is to grow a following online and build your online story. In your job search, your narrative is important. You want more professional content posted on the Internet, so people are reading the narrative you choose.

One thing to consider is deciding which social media networks to use for your transition. I tell people to not use more than three online platforms to professionally promote themselves. You are more than welcome to, but it will take up a lot of your time to keep each platform current. Also you should know that not all social media networks are created equal. We will go into detail about the different networks later in the chapter.

Factors to focus on as you formulate your strategy include the following questions:

Who is your target audience?

What social media platforms are you currently using?

How much time do you want to devote to social media?

Depending on how you communicate, what career field you are in, and if you are already on social media will determine what sites you prioritize. Personally I use LinkedIn, Facebook, and my third platform depends on what I post about, but it is usually Twitter, even though I'm not very active there.

You should have already created your avatar in the branding section (see "Rebranding Yourself" in Chapter 3), so you should have your audience narrowed down at this point. If you don't, continue to work on it until you have it to the lowest common denominator. You can't go too narrow at the start of your online life. Begin in your narrowest niche and expand from there as you gain a following.

When you look at your avatar, what site do you think he or she would use the most? That is the site you should focus on. If it is LinkedIn, which it most likely will be for a career transition, you need to completely fill out your profile on that site. I will break down your LinkedIn profile in the next section.

You already know what your message is and how you want to begin to get that message out. For example, I use LinkedIn to post my blog articles. This creates a dialogue with my network about issues they are having and helps me provide content that fills their needs. This also builds my reputation as being of value to my network in their job searches. It then brings more readers and attention to my website.

I make sure that my social media posts are only about opportunities and programs designed to assist veterans in their transition. I also mix in some content about leader development and veterans who have successfully transitioned from the military and how they did it. The main thing to remember, when it comes to choosing content for your main professional social media sites, is to not confuse your message. You only want to post content about the value you offer and your field of expertise.

To create that content, just post about what you know. You can adjust the pulse setting in LinkedIn to list news from your area of expertise. If you are not comfortable to create your own blog content, you can find news you have opinions about. Share the news story with your network and groups and add a paragraph of original thought about the story. This will show your knowledge without the process of creating 500–1,000 words for a full post.

If you do post original content, you can do so about once a week to begin until you find your groove. The more you write, the easier it gets. If you want to share a shorter post, you have to try to post something every day. I would recommend sharing a short post every day, even if you post original longer content weekly.

As I already stated, I recommend LinkedIn. It is a great place to interact with your professional network. The key is to engage your connections and show how you can add value to their lives. This will expand your job search, as you build trust within your network. If one of your connections comes across an employment position, they will think of you because you have shown what your area of expertise is and you are on people's minds.

There are many people who use Facebook as their main source of social media. This is fine, if you can build a base of followers on the site on a personal level. The good thing about Facebook is that there is more to it than posting videos and family pictures. You can either join a group or start your own group. I'm beginning a Facebook invite-only group for people being mentored through the *Crush You Military Transition* process. This will allow me to have one more place to engage a small portion of my audience and narrow conversations to further break down instructions, more than I can through the blog.

I use Facebook as my secondary social media site. When I post to my blog, I have a plug-in that automatically posts to all my social media sites. Even though my main network is through LinkedIn, I have military friends who I communicate with on Facebook and this gets my content to those in my closer circle. Those are the people who know that I can be trusted and they will share it with their friends and that extends my reach farther.

One way you can initially measure your success is by feedback. I have listed my contact information everywhere. I know that I posted good content when I receive questions to clarify information in the post or thanking me for the post. Trust me, if people are consuming your content and it is improving their lives, they will let you know.

What success is for you will depend on your mission and vision. You should use the goals section of the branding phase to define what you think success is. You are the only person who knows what you think success is.

In a 2013 survey, conducted by jobvite.com, 78 percent of the 860 recruiters asked said they use social media to hire candidates, and 92 percent of those recruiters use LinkedIn to hire job candidates compared to 24 percent using Facebook, and 14 percent using Twitter. In addition, 42 percent stated that what they saw on a candidate's social media had an effect on if they hired a person or not. Let's dive a little deeper into different social media sites to help you choose which are right for you.

Introduction to LinkedIn

LinkedIn is a site to connect professionals with other professionals, recruiters, and potential employers. A point benefit to know upfront is that any veteran or transitioning service member who has served one day of active service after September 11, 2001, can receive a free year of premium LinkedIn. I believe your LinkedIn profile is so critical that I put together a full tutorial in this section to walk you through the process.

There are a lot of people who don't know how to ask people to connect with other people they might not know. For our purposes here, the thing you want to remember is to personalize the invite. LinkedIn does put a default text in your message box. Erase it and personalize the message. For example, when I connect with a service member or veteran, I use the following invite. *Thank you for your service. I'd like to add you to my network. Have a great day.* This is all you need to break the ice and make a connection. Once I began using this, I jumped from 129 to 1,250 contacts in less than two months. For other people, simply read their profile and use information you have in common to ask for a connection. This is why people are on the site, consider it networking and meet people.

LinkedIn is used by recruiters who use the site to post open positions and find people who are available to take those jobs. I always connect with recruiters and maintain active communications with them. This way if someone in my network is looking for a job, I can pass their information along to the recruiters in my network to connect them.

Groups are also a great way to join and start professional discussions with likeminded people. This sharing of ideas creates relationships, and relationship building is what you should be focused on during your job search. Every person you can connect with is a possible lead for a position. If you don't find a group you want to join, you can create your own niche group.

LinkedIn Guide

As I said before, I get frustrated looking at LinkedIn. I see the same mistakes from veterans all the time, and I want to help them. I think it would be easier if people changed the way they look at their LinkedIn page. Here are some quick tips to take your page over the top.

We are going to pay the most attention to what first shows on your screen when you load your profile. Your picture, name, some job and education information, and your location. Not much to go off of, but this is the section you need to sell people on, so they want to read the rest of your profile.

Think of your LinkedIn profile like a newspaper. Now I am in no way coming up with the analogy on my own. I have heard this before from many people about basic webpage design. I think it is obvious that not enough people have heard it, so I'll use it too. When you see a newspaper on sale, you see what is displayed above the fold. This is where they sensationalize the major stories to get you to spend your money on the paper. In the same way, you have to sensationalize yourself in that above-the-fold section of your LinkedIn profile. Here are four of the things that you have to get right to impress people and let them know you are serious.

1. *Photo*

Not having a picture or wearing your uniform. You want to make a personal connection with people you are interested in connecting with. That is hard to do if people have to imagine what you might look like. If you don't have a photo, you also run the risk of people thinking you are spamming them or are hiding something. Ideally you will have a professional photo in proper attire with a white or other neutral background. You want to look inviting enough for someone to want to meet you. If you have a picture on your profile of you scowling, who would want to meet you? Show that big smile and invite people to connect with you.

2. *Headline*

You don't have to put your current job position in as your headline. Instead of "Logistics Officer," I have, "Logistics Leader and Mentor I Assisting Transitioning Veterans @ www.jphillipy.com." That is what I do to add value to people's lives. It doesn't matter the job that I'm currently working. I am a leader and mentor first and in my spare time I write a blog to assist transitioning veterans. I also inserted my website into the heading, because that is where I blog about programs and other tips and tricks to help veterans put their best foot forward.

I see the majority of military personnel with a jargon-filled headline. Change it to what you want to be defined as. You want to send a message that you are more than your current position. This does two things.

First, you will send the message that you are thinking about where you add value overall in a workplace. This allows people viewing your profile to see what talents you offer. **Second**, it shows you put thought into your life beyond the military, and you are serious and ready for your transition to civilian life. It is your job to prove you are not a military-brainwashed robot who cannot function outside the military.

3. LinkedIn URL

Under you photo, you will see your URL for LinkedIn. It is easy to personalize your URL. Rather than "www.LinkedIn.com/joe-e-martin-4359643" you can change it to "www.LinkedIn.com/joemartin." The personalized formatting looks better and makes it easier to find you. Just click on "edit profile" and hit edit next to your URL. That is really how easy it is. That little extra effort makes you more searchable and just shows you care to take care of the small details.

4. Summary

Finally, depending on your screen and settings, you might be able to see the very top of your profile summary. If you managed to get someone this far into your profile, you have a paragraph to convince them to scroll down farther and really learn who you are. This is your chance to hook the reader. Make sure this section is about what you can do for an employer.

Consider there might be hundreds of people looking for the same position that you are. Why should that employer hire you? Put your bottom line up front and sell yourself. You already did most of this work in previous chapters; simply tailor your message for your target industry.

Your profile doesn't have to begin with how awesome you are and all your accolades. It also should not just contain keywords or bullet statements of generalized achievements. Neither of those is inviting people to begin a digital conversation to get to know you better.

Introduction to Facebook

Facebook has about 150 million members in the United States, which is about 40 percent of the world's users. If used properly, it is a tremendous tool toward your job search. You do have to be cautious of Facebook in regard to what is posted on your site. If you have your profile set to super private, potential employers might think you are hiding things. However, if your Facebook page is completely open and you have your weekend drinking pictures showing, you are taking a big chance of hurting your search.

One tactic that I like to have people use is to use two different Facebook pages. I don't post crazy drinking pictures, because I am way past that phase. I do sometimes have people from my past who post wild photos on their pages. I use a fake name for my personal page and my proper name for my professional page. I do not add those "wild" people as friends on my professional page. This keeps my professional life and my private life separated. Not only that, but people I do business with don't necessarily need to see pictures of my family and my activities. That is the main reason I like having a buffer between my two sides of life.

Another advantage of Facebook is the ability to create a group that is focused toward what your area of expertise is. Make sure the page is linked to your personal brand and shares the key message you are trying to relay. You can use this Facebook page to share information about your career field and post original content you created about your knowledge to prove your value, rather than just talking about it.

Bottom line is if you are a responsible Facebook user, you can use the social media site to expand your network and get noticed by recruiters and employers. Again I would only post topics on your professional page that relate to your industry and comment on them with some original thought. This will help demonstrate your expertise and help get you noticed.

Introduction to Twitter

I'm not a big fan of Twitter for job searches, but a lot of people are on the site and you can connect with them to discover jobs. One thing to remember is you need to completely fill out your profile with your brand message. With Twitter, you are limited on the number of characters you can enter, so your profile is going to be even more critical than some of the other social media sites. The profiles here are used by recruiters to sift through people to see if they are relevant to a job opening. If you leave your profile blank, you are not offering them anything of value.

One tactic is to link your Twitter profile to your LinkedIn account or your personal website or blog. This will extend your reach and funnel your Twitter connections to your other social media locations, where they can learn more about you and form a deeper connection.

For Twitter, you are judged based on your number of followers. The more followers you have, the more credibility and authority you will have when people see your tweets. One way to gain more followers is to follow more people and allow their followers to see you. Another method is to retweet other people's tweets and include the original sender's name in the tweet. Then your retweet will appear in more Twitter timelines, increasing your visibility.

Here are some tactics to use to strengthen your Twitter account for your job search.

1. Make your username something unique that relates to you or your job search. I use @jeffreyphillipy, this makes it clear who I am when I connect with people. That is the same name I use for all my social media to make sure there is no confusion and my network can find me across all social media platforms.

2. Make your Twitter account name something relatable. I again use my full name for my Twitter account. I could use *Crush Your Military*

Transition, because my username is already my full name. This puts my name with this book in Twitter, allowing people to connect the dots and know it is me.

3. Make your Twitter photo the same head shot that you use across all social media platforms.

4. Fill your Twitter bio with keywords that describe you. Recruiters search for candidates with the skills and requirements that they are looking for. Search the positions you want online and use those keywords in your bio. This will also help your Twitter account get found via Google searches, increasing your visibility.

YouTube

YouTube is a great social media site for people who have the personality to promote themselves visually without seeming too awkward. This is a great site for free promotion. You can basically make a commercial about yourself. What better way is there to explain your value than producing YouTube videos about topics in your profession? Not only does this show your grasp on these subjects, but it also gives an example of your personality and communication skills.

One thing I heard sticks with me about networking.

**It's not what you know and
it's not who you know,
it's how well they know you.**

Networking is about making a personal connection. The more you make people feel like they really know you, the more opportunities you will get. When people see and hear you, they will feel closer to knowing you, and you will move higher on their list of candidates.

The YouTube site also allows you to show your creativity and get noticed as an innovator. It is a great place to experiment with new designs and processes. No matter what your profession is, employers are always looking for creative people. In the couple minutes that it takes to post a video, it just gives you one more opportunity to stand out and get discovered.

Another angle to use YouTube is watching company-created channels. These are video channels created by companies to discuss what's new and on the horizon in the company, what departments are expanding, and other related information. You can use these details to tailor your job search and look for information to use in job interviews to show you know the company. This is just another tool to get you in the door.

5 Networking

The number one point I want to get across to make you a better networker is to not be a taker. Focus on being seen as a giver. What do I mean by that? Many people view networking as a way to meet people who can help them. Do you like being used? That's what a lot of people do. When you meet someone, your first thought should be what you can do to add value to their life or business.

This will show the other person that you care enough to want to build a relationship. It is also just being a good person, which I think we have lost the art of throughout the years. Mr. Whoever from Company XYZ has people trying to get his time all day long, and the majority of those people are out for themselves. If you want to truly leave a memorable impression on Mr. Whoever, impress him by offering value to him rather than asking for something.

Networking is a limiting term to use, because you have to think about it as more than that. From now on when you hear the word "networking," I want you to translate that to "relationship building." It isn't about who you know or who knows you. The key to relationship building is who do you know well. As I said before, you need to look at every relationship you have as an opportunity to help people. If you help enough people, it will come back around to help you.

Your transition isn't a fulltime job, but networking is fulltime. Building and maintaining meaningful relationships is hard work. You really have to put time into showing the desire you have to make it work. You should spend time each day staying in contact with a couple of your connections. If you contact five people per day, five days a week, that's 25 people per week you are reaching out to. It doesn't have to be a long email, but there has to be some substance to it.

Better yet, if you can find a reason to call, instead of emailing, it is even better. With email and texting, phone calls are a lost art that can set you apart from the crowd with a personal touch. The point is when an opportunity comes up, your contacts are going to think of you, because you are engaging them on a regular basis.

When networking is done right, it is almost like dating. Both parties interact to see if there is any chemistry between them. You send emails and maybe connect with some phone calls. If you both see a future in the relationship, you make plans to meet and discuss taking your relationship to the next level.

Whether you are attending a dinner party or some other event, you need to have your every move calculated from the time you start getting ready to attend. You should have some idea of who is going to be there. Research them and gather enough information so you can maintain a good 5–10 minute conversation.

This is the ideal time for a social conversation. You want to be able to have enough time to pique the interest of the person you are talking to and exchange business cards. You also do not want to monopolize their time. You want to work your way around the event and mingle

I recommend *How to Work a Room*, by Susan RoAne. This is a great book to help you tactically approach networking. It is especially good for introverts, like me, who feel overwhelmed in social settings. This truly changed my whole approach, and I actually enjoy being social now. I even enjoy public speaking.

Please see the next page to begin working through your existing network. This will show you where your current network is strong and where it needs work. This will assist you in creating a plan of action to focus your networking toward landing a position in your desired industry.

Existing Network Map

Use this page to begin brainstorming people you already have in your network and analyzing the areas where your network needs improvement.

Friends/Relatives	Neighbors	Past Associates
Consultants	Former Employers	Lawyers
College Associates	Business Owners	Doctors
Community Leaders	People You Recently Met	Professional Associations

Culture Change

Unless you are planning on being a mercenary, your next career will be quite different from your time in the military. After discussing the subject with some newly discharged veterans, I found out what they were most frustrated about. In the military, there is a completely structured atmosphere where if you tell someone to complete a task it is going to get done. You will have to follow up and make sure it is going to be completed on time but it will be completed. The gripe I hear the most from ex-military personnel is that civilians don't have the same focus on accountability and consideration of deadlines that military personnel have ingrained in them.

This is something you should be ready for. The days where you have complete control are gone. You will have to be actively involved in the daily tasks to make sure everyone is pulling their weight. However, there are some things you can do to get prepared for the culture in your industry of choice before you exit the military. This will allow you the mental preparation for dealing with possible differences you will encounter.

I recommend you start attending functions and conferences in the industries that interest you. The initial intent is not focused toward networking, even though you will meet some people in your field of interest. The focus is getting involved to make sure you are actually interested when you see the types of people you will be working with and what the work really involves.

This will also give you an opportunity to learn some of the new jargon in the profession and what is coming in the future of the industry. You want to be able to talk about topics and ask questions that are relevant during interviews. As we will discuss later, being prepared is a must. You can also try to make contact with veterans who are currently working in the industry and find out what the most difficult adjustment was for them.

Mind Your Manners

You never know who you are talking to and who they know. I talked to a veteran recently who told me his networking story and how surprised he was. He spent months applying for jobs and going to interviews. There was promise, but nothing panned out. One day he was talking to a small business owner and just happened to begin talking about his transition from the service.

The man asked for his information, and the veteran gave it to him, thinking it couldn't hurt. The veteran never expected anything to come of it. One day he received a call about an interview for a position he didn't apply for, but the job was in line with the work he was searching for. The interview was with the vice president of the company, who was friends with the small business owner who had asked for his information.

The couple of minutes that the veteran spent talking to the stranger he was doing business with yielded more results than the work he had put in up to that point. He easily could have made the purchase and left, but the veteran took the time to have a personal conversation with someone, expecting nothing more. It just goes to show that you have to treat everyone with respect when you are having conversations with people. The person you are dealing with might not be important in your mind, but they very well could hold the key to your future.

Elevator Pitch

An elevator pitch is a speech used to sell or promote something in the length of a short elevator ride, 20–30 seconds. By this point you should understand how important it is to be able to sell yourself with confidence. That should include an elevator pitch. Why, you ask?

Part of your plan is to get involved in the civilian side of your sector before you complete your transition by attending conferences and other events to afford you the opportunity to build your network. People are busy during these events and don't have all day to speak with you. How impressed would they be if you could clearly and concisely explain how you bring value to the industry in less than a minute? That would leave them a couple of minutes to engage in meaningful conversation with you rather than you fumbling around for several minutes and having them be confused about you.

Elevator Pitch Exercise

I want you to write a one-page letter to a potential employer explaining what value you bring to the company and the industry. Take your time completing this and do your best to write a whole page, but not more. It is better if you can complete this in one sitting, but it is not a requirement.

Once you are finished I want you to take a couple of days to narrow the thoughts on that one page to one paragraph that conveys the same information. Then once you have your paragraph, take a couple more days and reduce the same information from one paragraph to one sentence.

You now have your elevator pitch that you can quickly share. If you have additional time, you can relate the longer paragraph version. However, if you have the chance to meet someone for only an instant, you now have your golden sentence to give them. This is what you use to hand someone your business card and your elevator pitch. If you can also get a page of information to someone as you hand them a business card, then I guarantee they will be impressed and they will use your card at some point.

6 Financial Planning

Financial Situation

When transitioning, your financial situation can close doors for you if you do not prepare. It should be a no brainer, the less debt you have, the less monetary stress you will have during your transition. You should know the minimum that you need to earn to live comfortably as a civilian. Download the budget exercise at crushyourtransition.com and determine what you think your current situation is.

As you work through this section of the chapter, use your budget sheet as both a financial reality check and a foundation to build your action plan. If you use the form digitally, you can manipulate the data to build your action plan.

Manage Your Expectations

Before you begin, there are some things I want you to keep in mind. No matter how successful you were in the military, you might need to take a step back when you begin your civilian career. That also means that there is a good chance you could earn less money when you do get a new job. Not only could you earn less, but you likely will be required to pay more taxes.

In the military, most allowances were tax free, and you might not have been required to pay state taxes while you served. These variables will need to be factored in when you figure out your financial situation in this section. Factor your current pay from your base pay. You will be better off than if you use your basic allowance for housing and other extra benefits when comparing current military part to what you expect to make in your post-military career.

Analyze Your Current Situation

Take some time and gather the following items:

- 6–12 months of bank statements
- 6–12 months of credit card statements
- highlighters in various colors
- last year's tax return
- the last two leave and earnings statements or paystubs for you and your spouse.

Use these items to fill out your budget worksheet and be honest about where your money is going. Then, on a separate sheet of paper, break your expenses into three categories.

Essential: This includes expenses that cover food, clothing, housing, transportation, and health care.

Non-Essential: cable, cell phone, gym memberships, subscriptions, and other items you receive bills for.

Required Non-Monthly Expenses: property taxes, insurance premiums, auto registration, home warranties, and others that might come due once a year. Be sure to take these periodic expenses and calculate their cost on a monthly basis and include these figures in your post-military budget.

Next, you have to remember that you are transitioning from a job where you received free health care, for the most part. Those expenses will now have to be added to your budget. That includes premiums for health insurance, dental, vision, and any other expenses to include co-pays and prescriptions. Be sure to shop around for your health care, and if you have a doctor you like, ask about ways to cut the cost of your current care. There might be programs your medical provider participates in and you just don't know about them.

To continue breaking down your expenses, list your extra expenses or what a lot of people call the "miscellaneous fund." These expenses include trips, vacations, sports, entertainment, and other "fun" items. After you do this, make a list of how you expect to live during your transition.

No matter how marketable you think you are, you might have a couple of months before you receive a job offer. The thing you need to remember is that there are a number of veterans out there right now looking for employment. There is inherently nothing special about you. It is your job to sell yourself. Think about where you are willing to reallocate money in order to save more during your transition.

1. Add up your fixed expenses (essential and required).

2. Add up your non-essential expenses.

3. Total these two expenses together.

4. Divide your fixed expenses (from step 1) by your total expenses (step 3) to determine the percentage of your expenses that are a monthly requirement.

5. Deduct the percentage that you arrived at in step 4 from 100. This will give you an idea about the percentage of your income that you currently have available to work with. The further you are from your transition date, the better this process will serve you.

Once you decide on a budget, you need to decide how you are going to record your budget going forward. You need to keep yourself honest, and to do that you need to write down what you spend, by how it fits into your budget. In the beginning, you need to weekly reconcile your spending against your budget. Eventually you can move that to monthly, once you get on a routine. The idea behind this is that wallets are like kids: if you don't control them, they will run wild and cause problems.

The new word I want you to learn is "no." When you or your spouse wants something that goes against the budget, you will say no. When you want something that goes against the budget, your spouse needs to tell you no. A budget is no different from a diet. If you are part of a couple, you both need to be onboard with the plan. It's going to be hard to lose 30 pounds if your spouse is eating pizza and drinking beer every night. A budget is no different and a little sacrifice today can add tremendous dividends down the road.

Let me clear up a common misconception. Tracking your spending is not budgeting. Budgeting consists of having targets and goals weekly or monthly that define your spending. You might think you are tracking what you are spending, but if you're not defining what is supposed to go out and comparing that with your statements showing what actually went out, you are not budgeting and you are not working toward your goals.

Paying Off Your Debt

I always encourage people to be debt free. My wife and I were determined to get to the point where we were debt free and stay that way. Just to be clear, I do have a mortgage. I don't think that is an issue because it is an investment. I'm talking about things such as car payments, taking a loan for an recreational vehicle, and other non-essential items. If you have a BMW with an $800 monthly car payment, you might look cool. But you could have paid for a Mazda for a third of the cost.

Your debt can hold you back from taking advantage of opportunities. In four years we got to the point where we were debt free with $100,000 in the bank. It wasn't easy, and we did sacrifice, but our life has been a lot less stressful from that point. We both have new cars and paid cash to save on the interest. Yes, that decreased our savings but without having car payments, we built the bank account back up. I just want you to know that I have seen this work.

To start the process, list all your bills that you need to pay off from lowest to highest with the minimum payment. This will allow you to clearly evaluate the problem and what you need to get paid off. Look at the remaining bills that you have, such as cable, cell phone, and other non-essential items.

Determine where you can sacrifice as you prepare for your transition. Is it worth not having the ridiculously big cable package and going with a basic plan to have a less stressful transition two years from now? That is up to you, but see where you can save some money and apply that to the lowest bill you need to pay off. Just remember that some companies require you to specify that the extra money in the payment is supposed to go toward the principal.

After you pay off the lowest bill, apply what you were paying on that bill to the next one on the list. As you pay more bills off, the momentum builds and you begin to see the light at the end of the tunnel. Trust me; once you get there it will be worth the little bit that you sacrificed to make it happen. Once you have these bills paid off and you are debt free, you can move that money to begin paying yourself to save.

How much do you have to save? That is up to debate. How marketable do you honestly believe you will be? Look back at the work you did when you were evaluating your skills, compared to the types of positions you desire. Do you need additional education or skills that require some extra training? Start researching whether there are any programs that can give you those skills for free or if you can volunteer and learn the skills without a formal certification.

I personally recommend a six- to eight-month emergency fund. This is not your checking account. You need to have a separate fund that is strictly for emergencies. This will give you a cushion during your transition, in case your car breaks down, you need house repairs, or there is a major medical emergency. If you're not prepared for these situations prior to your exit from the military, you might be stuck solving problems with your credit cards. That situation will only compound your problems and add to your stress during an already demanding time.

7 Building Your Résumé

"If I had more time, I would have written a shorter letter."
—Benjamin Franklin

This is the quote you need to keep in mind as you write your résumé. Make every word you use add value, and use your words to construct your thoughts as concisely as possible. You already thought about where you want to work and what you want to do. This is a necessary first step to write a targeted résumé to send to specific employers. People looking to get hired have less of a chance of receiving a response from hastily and randomly sent out generic résumés. You already designated the positions you are best qualified for, so let's begin writing your résumé.

I have seen a lot of really bad résumés from military people, and I blame a lot of that on the military Transition Assistance Program. I'm here with a systematic approach to get you on the right track. If you have not completed the worksheets from the skills portion of this book (see Chapter 2), do not collect your $200, and do not pass go. That process is critical for you to gain the self-awareness to write a great résumé.

One page is the ideal length for a résumé. You can get away with using more than a page, but never more than two. If you decide to use more than the one page, limit both the size of the second page header and how much of your data spills onto the second page.

Some things to be aware of include the following:

1. To keep your résumé concise, scrutinize every word to make sure it is necessary and adds value to the information.

2. Make sure to sell yourself in the first half of the page.

3. Don't staple the pages. This makes the résumé difficult to copy.

You can see above how we funnel your strengths into the résumé to make you a stronger candidate. Breaking the task into steps allows you to take the process into smaller steps, dissecting your talents to maximize your potential. Now if you want to do the skills tests again and put a little more effort into it, do it now before you continue with this chapter. There are free printable sheets at crushyourtransition.com.

First Draft

To get started, you don't need to worry about formatting. Think of this as more of a scratch pad. Later you can format a document and cut and paste from your draft. Here are the sections you're going to need.

1. Contact Information: Name, Address, Email Address (try to use an email address with your name in it, such as jeffreyphillipy@gmail.com), and website, if you have a personal site to promote your work or achievements.

2. Goals Statement: A goals statement could be used if you are transitioning careers. A statement as simple as this would be fine. "Transitioning to establish a career in the XYZ field."

3. Work History: Review your relevant history in reverse order, most recent to oldest. List job title, company name, location, and years/months you worked there. When you list the time you worked, January 2013–January 2015 would be written 1/13–1/15. The only month you will use a 0 for is 10 for October. Limit the employer address to city and state. The goal is to maximize room for the important information.

The debate still rages about how to list your achievements: paragraph form or bullet points. I prefer bullet points with 3 to 5 major achievements per position. My belief is that a paragraph makes readers feel like they have to read more. Bullet points can be skimmed quickly. You have 6–7 seconds for a hiring manager to get interested enough in your résumé to want to read more.

Make sure to start each point with a powerful action verb. Use present tense for your current position and past tense for your previous positions. You can also address any additional knowledge developed during that time or promotions. Make sure to use the skills you listed as your strengths when discussing your achievements, as they relate to this position. (You did most of the work already during the skills section.)Make sure you articulate your responsibilities and your achievements.

4. Education: Degrees and institutions you graduated from and include any professional certifications you received, if they relate to the position you are applying for.

Ok now that we have the draft complete, we are going to get ready to review it and enhance it. You have to remember that a lot of times your résumé will be the deciding factor on whether you get an interview or not. This is your one shot to make a good first impression, so spend the time and do it right. This is a good time to double-check that your résumé matches the qualifications listed for the specific position you are applying for.

**Just a note, if you are applying for more than one position at the same company, be careful about how different your résumés are. I still recommend crafting them to the specific position, but don't apply for the head accountant position and also apply for the lead marketer saying you are an expert in both positions.

Get through this brainstorming phase and take a minute and reflect on your draft. Read it and think about who you are. Can you identify yourself in a 30-second elevator speech? Practice if you can with friends. Go introduce yourself to people if you have to.

Now It's Time to Create

If you want to save time I do have multiple résumé formats to use and you can just input your data. I have tested these formats with different recruiters to make sure the forms can be trusted. Just make sure you have worked the draft enough to have your best work on the final product. The hard part is done, now it's just the formatting and tweaking.

This is where your military time adds value to your writing. We are already conditioned to write strong bullet points on evaluations and awards. You just have to put in the work to use the proper terms for your industry. You can do this and rock your résumé.

Refine this document until it is a work of art. If someone gets your résumé and it looks bad, it won't make the cut. There are some positions with 500–1,000 people applying for one job. You have been taught to know your audience. Make sure you know what the hiring manager is looking for. There is nothing wrong with calling the human resources section of the company and ask what they normally look for on résumés and what sections are weighted higher. Sometimes a little digging and asking the right questions will take you a long way.

Make sure that once you are complete, you give your résumé to a couple of people you trust to have them proofread it for you. Spell check is well and good, but it won't catch mistake like "from vs. form" or "two vs. to or too." Multiple proofreaders can also help to wordsmith your work making it more clear and concise. You are going to send your résumé to many people to read, so wouldn't it be better to get the opinion of others before the people who matter read it?

The following checklist is from theladders.com for advice on weaving your way through hiring systems that use the Applicant Tracking System to screen résumés. If you are applying through a system like this, pay attention so you don't get lost.

Checklist

1. Do not apply to a company multiple times if the positions do not match your experience and skills. Recruiters notice multiple submissions, and it reflects poorly on a candidate if he or she applies for jobs that aren't a good fit.

2. Don't send your résumé as an attachment. To avoid getting caught by security scans, paste the text into the body of the e-mail.

3. When e-mailing a résumé, keep exclamation marks out of the subject line and body of the text.

4. When e-mailing a résumé, don't use words in the document or headline that could be misinterpreted by spam filters. For example, use "graduated with high honors" instead of "graduated cum laude."

5. Include a professional or executive summary at the top of the résumé, followed by a list of bulleted qualifications and/or achievements.

6. Customize the professional/executive summary and bulleted list(s) with keywords that match a given job.

7. Make sure the keywords in the executive summary and bulleted qualifications and achievements replicate those in the job posting.

8. Keywords alone aren't enough. State-of-the-art ATS technology also relies on contextualization. Frame keywords with descriptive material that demonstrates experience and familiarity with the subject.

9. Do not use abbreviations, such as "Mgr" for "Manager." It is unlikely that the ATS has been programmed with a list of abbreviations to stand in for keywords.

10. Avoid misspellings. A misspelled keyword is one that the ATS will miss, lowering your ranking.

11. Use standard capitalization, not all lowercase or full capitals. Improper capitalization annoys recruiters.

12. Fill in all the information requested by an online application process, even if it's listed as optional. Recruiters often sort by optional information to filter out applicants, and filling in all fields will ensure you don't erroneously get caught in a screening filter.

13. Fill in all information requested by an online application process, even if it's included in your résumé. This information can be used to filter out applicants before a hiring manager comes to the point of opening the résumé itself.

14. If you're being referred by an employee, make sure the ATS knows it, because it's smart enough to care and will rate your résumé higher.

15. If the ATS offers options, opt for uploading your résumé instead of cutting and pasting. This feature often parses information and saves it in the optimal format, ensuring the cleanest presentation.

16. To avoid choking an ATS with a highly formatted résumé, make sure your résumé is in a clear, concise format, with your contact information located at the top instead of in the header or footer.

17. Do not include graphics or logos on a résumé; they can garble the information the ATS processes.

18. Respond within 24 hours after hearing from a company.

19. Keep an eye on your spam folders. Filters are so sensitive today that they can recognize e-mail that's automatically generated—a category which both spam and follow-up e-mail generated from an ATS program can fall into.

20. Adhere to instructions provided in a follow-up e-mail. If the follow-up e-mail lacks a phone number but directs you to respond with your availability, respond via e-mail, not by calling. This will likely get you the fastest response.

21. If you receive an automatically generated rejection e-mail, immediately contact the recruitment office of the rejecting organization or a sympathetic administrative assistant—anyone who can advise you as to the best way to replace the résumé currently in the ATS with one containing better keywords and phrases.

22. When reapplying after an initial rejection, tweak executive summaries and bulleted lists of key skills and achievements. Don't alter your work-history elements.

23. When reapplying, don't try to use a different e-mail address from the one you used on your first try. This isn't enough to avoid a duplicate record in advanced systems, such as Taleo, which use multiple candidate identifiers, so make sure to follow step 21.

24. Once your customized résumé has been resubmitted, contact the appropriate recruiter (or sympathetic administrative assistant) and request that your updated résumé be reviewed for the open position.

Résumé Example

Jeffrey Phillipy

222 Ford Rd, 1st St Roswell NM 12345 – 123-456-7890

jeffreyphillipy@jphillipy.com – www.jphillipy.com

Summary: Adept at budgeting, forecasting, supplier negotiations, and all elements of logistics management.

Work Experience:

All About Logistics Warehouse Supervisor 2/14 – Present

- Managed a highest volume warehouse in NM with over 400 customers and 1,000 shipments /week.

- Maintained 100 percent accountability for $55M in property over two years

- Managed schedules for 65 employees on three shifts.

Movertown Distribution Transportation Manager 3/11 – 2/14

- Initiated an improved maintenance program increasing vehicle readiness from 80 percent to 95 percent.

- Supervised 130 employees in 3 states with 100 percent delivery accuracy

- Outperformed every transportation manager in every region, earning manager of the year recognition.

Joe's Supply Service Stock Manager 10/08 – 1/14

- Designed new inventory process increasing accountability accuracy by 30 percent

- Trained new employees on all process and procedures

- Earned employee of the month five times for process improvements

Education

Newton University, MA Transportation Management 1/09 – 6/12

AM University, BA Management 8/04 – 6/08

Certification Six Sigma Black Belt 10/13 – 1/14

Skills: Project management, process improvement, team building, proficient in MS Office

What to Remember

You have to stress what you did well. For the most part, veterans are going to be able to get a job based on experience. Therefore, it is my opinion that your experience needs to be the first item on your résumé. That being said, there is no right answer. Every company looks for different things. That is why I recommend calling the HR department or networking with someone who works for the company to see what you need to do with your résumé. You will find 100 different formats for résumés and that is because your résumé needs to show your personality. This is your ad for your marketing campaign.

I have cover letters and résumé formats at crushyourtransition.com. For cover letters, I recommend them being short, if you even need one.

Federal Résumés

Federal résumés are different enough to have them in their own section in this chapter. As discussed, the average length of a private sector résumé is about one page. Federal résumés are roughly three pages, and if you are building your résumé on a site, such as usajobs.com, you could reach as many as five pages.

Let's look at some of the differences in the federal résumé format. The following are some of the details that are required:

Social Security Number
Supervisor's Names
Supervisor's Phone Numbers
Starting and Ending Salary
Employer Addresses
GPA
Related Coursework
Professional Memberships
Volunteer Service
Publications

When applying to work in the federal system, you want to make sure you're carefully reading the job posting. Your résumé will be screened for keywords. This will be a big part of the process of determination for who gets the interview. Read through the job listing and description to pull out keywords. Highlight them and as you edit your résumé, ensure you are using those keywords to tie your skills and experience to the posting.

As you do this, focus on the duties, qualifications, and requirements sections. This is where you are going to make your mark. Make your words count and really focus on this. You can be the most qualified applicant, but if you don't properly sell yourself, you are going to end up in the shredder. Make sure when you are matching keywords to your skills, you are also quantifying your achievements. Use numbers, percentages, and data to create the story of your positive impacts of past accomplishments and the impact you can have for the agency you are applying to.

One method to do this is to use what is referred to as the STAR system—Situation, Task, Action, Result. This will help you shape the narrative into an interesting story, which will pull the reader in to want to learn more. It will also assist you in making the story concise, as we talked about.

Think of a situation you were in, the tasks you had to complete to work through the situation, the actions you had to take to work through the tasks, and then describe the results. This will display your depth of experience. Make sure these are true events, because you will need to explain further when you get the interview.

Provide as much information as possible, but be clear and concise. This is not an easy process. Have people you trust proofread your résumé and edit it to show your complete abilities and be sure it's not too wordy. This will make you stand out by showing the hiring manager you have quality written communication skills.

Keep in mind that when you apply through the federal system, you will have to complete a job questionnaire. This is basically a test to verify your résumé. This is one reason you want to sell yourself on the résumé, but you have to be honest at the same time. Many people score themselves as less qualified than they really are. Most likely in the beginning of the questionnaire, there will be a warning telling you that if you do not answer truthfully you can be fired, imprisoned, or fined. This makes people timid when answering questions. If you have the qualifications they are asking about, let them know you are qualified. I can't say it enough, you cannot sell yourself short.

If you are applying for multiple positions, do not just cut and paste from your template résumé. You can paste your general information, but you have to change the key elements for each position. The qualifications, requirements, and duties need to reflect each position. This is where the bulk of your time will be spent. Take your time and pay attention to detail, or you won't make it past the computer screening.

8 The Interview

What to Wear

Men's Wardrobe Basics

I know I wasn't the world's best dresser. I blame this on my clothes being picked out for me by the military for my entire career. I know I'm not the only person with this issue. Think about this when you read this section. Hiring managers will tell you, if two or three applicants are close after the interview, the clothing and appearance can be the deciding factor. I don't want you to crush the interview and lose the job because of your attire. So let's go through what you will need to get started during your transition.

Everyone should have at least two, if not three, professional outfits before they begin their transition. You can get a couple basic items and go a long way on a moderate budget. Plan ahead and buy these items over time to piece some mix-and-match outfits together. This will have you looking like a long-time professional, allowing you to focus on the interview rather than worrying about what to wear.

Let's break down what a wardrobe should consist of beginning with the **suit jacket.** When choosing a suit for interviews you need to stay on the conservative side. For colors, I recommend charcoal, light gray, or brown with a two-inch lapel. A rule to remember is that slim lapels are more modern and wide lapels are more of a classic look. If you want to go with a formal business look for your interview, choose a double-button jacket with a notched lapel. Finally, you should make sure the jacket just covers the zipper of your pants. If you want to make a good impression on a budget, you can buy a nice off-the-rack suit but you should get it tailored to make sure it fits your body well.

The fit is something to pay attention to. Here are a couple easy things to look for when buying a jacket. The shoulders should lay flat with the seam on top as long as the shoulder and the suit sleeve should meet right where the arm connects to your shoulder. The shoulder is the hardest part of a suit to have adjusted so make sure you check before you buy.

There should not be a gap between the collar and the lapel. The collar of your suit should rest against your shirt collar, which should lie against your neck. In the arms, you should not have a lot of excess material, and you should be able to slide your hand between your chest and the jacket comfortably, but not with a lot of space in between. Close the top button of the suit and check to make sure it closes easily and there are no wrinkles from being too light. Also check the bottom of the front of the suit, the material can separate slightly but you shouldn't be able to see any of your shirt. In the back the jacket should end where the buttocks begin to curve back in toward the legs.

Moving to your **suit pants,** pay attention to make sure you don't have a lot of extra fabric that bunches. The bottom of your pants should just touch the top of your shoe, creating a subtle dimple or crease in the bottom front of your pants. The bottom of the pants in the back can fall a little lower, but shouldn't fall past the heel. The buttocks should have the fabric lay over the curve of your body without pulling and sagging. If it is a good fit, the pants should have just a little room between the fabric and the underwear.

Leather **shoes** with thin leather soles are what you want to wear with your suit. Rubber soles do not look professional.

When it comes to the rest of your items, if you have trouble coordinating colors, make sure the store has someone knowledgeable and ask for help. I will discuss some color schemes below. The **shirt** you wear with your suit should fit well—get measured for your correct size. The sleeves of the shirt should extend roughly a half inch beyond the sleeve of the suit.

Match the width of the **tie** to the width of your lapel, and make sure it falls so it just touches your waistline. The knot for your tie depends on the size of your head. Bigger heads require a full Windsor and slimmer heads call for a half Windsor. Ensure your tie is a darker color than your shirt. You want to go bold with your tie, as it's the first thing people notice.

Yes, your shoe color should match your **belt** color and if your pants fit properly you don't need to wear a belt.

Top it all off with a nice **watch**.

Color Schemes

Charcoal suit: Cream shirt with a blue stripe tie

Red pencil stripe shirt with a navy stripe tie

Solid white shirt with a solid black tie

Light Gray: Red and white checkered shirt with a solid burgundy tie

White shirt with a navy tie

Navy bengal stripes with a solid navy tie

Brown: White shirt with a navy polka-dot tie

Blue window pane with a burgundy paisley tie

Gray checkered shirt with a brown and gray tie

Women's Wardrobe Basics

I also want to cover interview clothing for females. When purchasing a wardrobe, you want to make sure you have the correct fit. If you're on a budget, look for items that you can also wear to dress down.

Here are some basic fitting tips for purchasing your items. The **blazer** should fit comfortably on the shoulders without pulling, with the seams centered on top. Make sure the shoulders don't extend past where the arm meets the shoulder. Check the fit at the widest part of your body (shoulders, chest, or waist). If your shoulders are the widest part, you can tailor the rest of the blazer for a better fit. The length is mostly based on your height; petite women can go with a cropped blazer, where taller women might be better with a longer style. The sleeve should extend to the wrist bone unless you will be wearing a long sleeved shirt, then it should only extend to just above the wrist bone.

When trying on **pants,** make sure you sit down. The waist should be comfortable. If they are tight, go with a bigger size and have them taken in. Check the front of the pants and the crotch area to make sure there is no pulling. If they are too baggy in the legs, have them tailored for a slimmer look. You have to know the height of your heel to have the pants altered correctly. The hem should just graze the floor but not drag. For a more modern look, the front of your pants should just touch the top of the shoe, causing a slight break or dimple in the seam of the leg.

If you choose to go with a pencil **skirt,** the waist should sit at or just below your natural waist. The navel can be used for a guide. You should not have your skirt be too tight; the zipper should be easily zipped with you relaxed. Use the three-way mirror to check the thigh area. There should not be any pulling or extra fabric that bunches. The material should flow nicely against your body with room to move. The hem should fall to the knee or just above

Finally, a sheath **dress** is perfectly acceptable for interview attire. The neckline should fall just below your collarbone. Be sure to lean forward when you are trying it on, to make sure you don't expose excessive cleavage. The bust should fit with no gapping, and you should be able to rotate your arms with your bra remaining fully covered. The flow of the dress should taper in to flatter your figure, with the hem falling just above the knee. Like the skirt, you should not have tightness or excessive material in the waist or hips.

To close your wardrobe, your **heels** should not be higher than three inches, and you should only wear them if you are good at walking in them. Use a moderate size **handbag** that matches your shoes. Limit your **jewelry** to three pieces: earrings, necklace, and watch. Also make sure you don't jingle. If you wear **perfume** it should be a very light scent, but you are better off not wearing any.

Below are some outfit ideas:

1. Start with a basic black suit with a wool material, so it is suitable for multiple seasons with the ability to transition easily from day to night use.

2. To go with the suit, purchase a matching black skirt for a more formal look and the matching black pants. This way you have them all at the same time and you don't end up with three shades of black from purchasing them separately.

3. For tops, you are safe choosing a cream or off-white shell top and a gray silk blouse. This maintains your mix-and-match ability. For example, you can wear the jacket with a pair of jeans, the gray top with the skirt or the pants without the jacket, and the shell top with the skirt, pants, or jeans.

4. To add to the collection, you can get a black modern-style pin-dot jacket and a black shift dress. This gives you another option you can wear together, and you can lose the jacket for an easy transition from day to

night. The jacket will also match your other items to maximize your outfit choices on a budget.

5. Finally, if you have a little room left in your budget, you can get a black jacket with pinstripes and soften it up with the gray silk blouse. When worn with the skirt, it will give you a strong look for any interview.

Preparing for the Interview

When you walk into an interview, the hard part is finished. That is the performance you have been getting ready to give. You need to do your homework to make sure that is the situation for you. We already completed some of that by deciding what positions you are most qualified for to not struggle with your job campaign. You learned how to dress appropriately on a budget. So let's look at what is required to get you ready for the interview.

Begin by looking at the five companies that you wanted to work for when you completed your skills evaluation. List those companies in the order you want to work for them. Begin with the one you want to work for the most. You need to Google the company or just go to the company website and begin your research. Yes, research, you need to do it.

Remember this is a job campaign, not a job search. That means you are taking a proactive approach to make things happen, rather than waiting for something to happen. What does that mean for you? The beginning is to get a general overview to understand the company.

How is this company going to help you meet your career goals, and what can you do for this company? Rather than just looking for a job, there should be a point to why you want to work there. Trust me, as I will cover a little later, if you don't really care about working at the organization, it will show during the interview. This is one reason that people have 75 interviews and no job.

If you find that the company can benefit from your goals, your next step is to begin digging into the company's past. One of the questions you will most likely be asked is "Why do you want to work here?" What is a better answer? Something that you might have found on the front page of the website or on Yahoo that morning or an answer from the lineage of the company? The interview is a competition of who wants to work there more. Unless you get off the couch, you are not going to win the Boston Marathon. You have to put in the long hours on the road and in the gym. You need to think about your interview the same way. You are working out to be the winner in this race.

Start taking notes:

How long has the company existed?

How have the mission, vision, and products changed from the beginning versus today?

Have the core aspects of the company changed?

What major milestones has it achieved?

Who were the founders of the company?

Once you have your notes, go through them and figure out how the information you found relates to your goals and your identity in the industry. Look for common themes that you can use to answer possible interview questions.

Following the past, you want to move into the present to perform the same drill again. Go through the company website and see how the current structure of the company and products or projects fit into your skills to assist the company. This will tie into the interview process we will discuss later in this section.

When looking at the present information about the company, you cannot forget about social media accounts. Go to the LinkedIn, Facebook, and Twitter sites to see what kind of presence the company has. Connect with some people from the company on social media and engage them to learn more about both the company and how the hiring process works. You can never have enough information.

Other information to look for in regard to present information includes the financials, leadership structure, room for growth in your industry, and recent press releases. If you want to work for this company, you want the interviewers to get the feeling of how bad you want to work there. While you are answering interview questions, you will be tying in information from the company. This will give you credibility, because the interviewers will see that you know and understand how the company is set up and how you will fit in. This research will also help you formulate questions to ask at the end of the interview.

What to Take to the Interview

1. Print a couple of copies of your résumé. Use good paper, and have crisp copies ready on request. Put them in a binder or notebook to keep them in good condition. You want them as nice as possible.

2. Take your research and prep work with you to the interview. There is nothing wrong with referring to your notes to ask a question or to bring something into the conversation that you remembered reading. It is going to show the interviewer you did your homework. Just make sure your notes are organized. You do not want to be stumbling through several loose pages, showing you are unorganized.

3. Make sure you have some blank paper to take additional notes. You do not want to be scribbling notes through the entire interview, but you might want to write down any key points or contact information.

4. Take a snack. Almonds, protein bar, or any other non-messy snack will ensure that hunger does not distract you during the interview.

5. Take mints and water. You want to make sure that your breath does not distract your interviewer. Bad breath can be a deal breaker.

Psychological Tactics to Appear Confident

1. Arrive 10–15 minutes early, this will allow you to compose yourself, look at your notes, and check in to verify you are in the right location.

2. If it is cold outside or you are nervous, use the bathroom to wash your hands with warm water. If there is an air dryer use it to dry and warm your hands. If your hands are warm and dry, you will appear more confident. Cold and clammy hands are a sign that you are nervous.

3. Take your time when you answer the interview questions. Taking a second or two in order to compose yourself before answering will help you seem more confident. Spilling out an answer too quickly and not well spoken can make you appear nervous.

4. Visualize yourself crushing the interview. You know you put in the work to prepare for this moment. Be confident in your ability to take care of business and see yourself getting the job.

Conduct during the Interview

There are some key things to remember during the interview. Employers said that 55 percent of the time they know within the first 90 seconds if they are interested in a candidate. The first impression can kill you in an interview. Don't go through all the hard work to lose it so fast.

1. Smile and give a firm handshake. Be sure to let the interviewer initiate the handshake. Firm does not mean to crush the interviewer's hand.

2. During the interview, address the interviewer with the name that they used to introduce themselves.

3. Maintain a balanced conversation. You need to engage the answers with energy, but do not control the conversation. There is no need to tell your life story. Make your answers concise and to the point, the last thing you want to do is ramble through the interview.

4. Remember to use your manners. This should go without saying, but you need to be polite and maintain a good posture throughout the interview.

5. Do not ask about the pay, vacation, or benefits during the interview.

6. In the section before this, I said to bring mints to the interview. Do not bring gum, which can distract the interviewer. If you need a mint, be sure it's not still in your mouth before you start the interview.

7. Be sure that you have no distracting mannerisms, such as cracking your knuckles, playing with your hair, or excessive hand gestures. These actions will take the focus off of what you are saying and direct the interviewer's attention to what you are doing.

Answering Interview Questions

Here is a look at 21 of the most asked questions in job interviews. I'm also adding some guidelines to answer them. The crazy thing is that questions that should be easy are some of the hardest to answer. Are you prepared to give an answer to: "Tell me about yourself"? Practice giving answers to the following topics.

1. Tell me about yourself. Keep the answer related to the company and job you are interviewing for. If you have a hobby or pastime, do not discuss it unless it relates to the position.

2. Tell me about your dream job. Again, keep the answer aimed toward the company you are applying for. If your dream job is to be a computer game programmer and you're applying for an industrial engineer position, that dream job isn't going to help you get the job.

3. Why did you leave your last job? If you are leaving the military, keep the answer positive and geared toward seeking more challenging opportunities.

4. What are some of your weaknesses? Have a couple of small things that you found challenging in your last position and talk about what you did to improve those weaknesses. Do not go straight to your bad choices in relationships or drug use.

5. What are your strengths? Do not make yourself sound like you can conquer the world. Think back to what you have been complimented on and projects you have excelled in. Have a couple of examples ready that show you are ready to take on the position you are interviewing for.

6. What do you know about our company? This is why you did the research. Anyone can give a simple answer, but you will have one with some thought behind it.

7. Why should we hire you? Use a calm, balanced tone and give a sincere answer that lets the interviewer know you want to work there, as much as the company needs you to work there.

8. Do you consider yourself to be a success? Yes, you do! Discuss your achievements and your education, compared to your work experience. Relate a situation where you had to overcome obstacles to succeed.

9. Why do you have a large employment gap? Turn the question around and discuss what you did in that time to improve yourself and your skills. Make sure you have an answer if you do have a work gap.

10. What do coworkers say about you? You already answered this in your branding section and should be able to craft an answer. If you skipped it, go back and go through that section in Chapter 3.

11. How long do you see yourself working here? Don't specify a timeline. You see yourself working there as long as the relationship is beneficial to both parties.

12. Describe your management style. Describe situations where you led projects and communicated with subordinates, peers, and senior leaders.

13. Are you a team player? Yes, give examples of successful team projects you were a part of.

14. Describe your work philosophy. Try not to use adjectives to talk about this. Discuss your basic work ethic that you used in your past position. Make sure you do it with energy and enthusiasm.

15. Do you think you are overqualified for this position? Just reiterate why you are the right person for the job.

16. What position do you want on a team: leader or follower? Explain that the success of the project is what is important and if someone more knowledgeable leads, you have the flexibility to follow, but you are always comfortable leading.

17. Why would you do well at this job? Describe the skill sets you have and how you would add value to the company.

18. Do you think you have a lack of experience? Give an experience where you performed similar jobs and how your current skills helped you succeed.

19. What motivates you? Think of a motivational answer that deals with work environments, discipline, and integrity.

20. What is your five-year plan? Have an answer that relates to the company you are applying with. Make sure you are giving an answer that shows you have vision and a plan for your future.

21. How do you handle criticism? You think it is the best way to improve, and you never take it personally.

Interview Tactics

Here are some tactics to help you answer the interview questions and make more of an impact.

1. You want to make sure you are giving honest answers. You can explain not having enough education or experience, but there is no explaining dishonesty. Maintain your integrity.

2. Try to find something in common with the interviewer. If you are being interviewed in the interviewer's office, see if there is anything to bond with them. School, family, sports team, etc., or any common bond can lighten the mood a little and help you relax. A personal connection will make the interviewer feel as if they know you better.

3. During the interview preparation, always have examples. Practice the answers to as many questions as you can, until you feel comfortable and you can talk about concise and relevant situations that help put substance in your answers.

4. No one is going to believe you, if you make yourself sound perfect. Be humble in your responses. You can show you are confident and will add value to the company, instead of coming across as conceited.

5. No matter how informal the interviewer seems, do not let that throw you off. Maintain you professionalism and remain confident and polite. It could always be a test, but you can never go wrong remaining professional.

6. A study at the University of California revealed the most powerful words in the English language are: discovery, guarantee, love, proven, results, save, easy, health, money, new, safety, and you. Practice using them.

Best Questions to Ask the Interviewer

The best questions to ask during an interview will show that you did your own research and that you understand the company. The goal is to do whatever you can to subtly display your desire to work for this company. Below is a list of good questions to ask after the interviewer is done. Questions need to have some substance to them, as anyone can pull something from the Internet on the morning of the interview. Show you put your work in and get this job.

1. What is the normal hiring timeline, and what are they looking for personally in a candidate? This gives you an opportunity to show why you fit in the company's culture, which you wouldn't normally have had the opportunity to share.

2. Ask about the status of a current project. This relates to what you learned from your research that is relevant to the section you are applying for. This will demonstrate that you have knowledge of the area you want to work in.

3. Ask about the company culture, or how work assignments are handed out? This demonstrates your interest to know more about the day-to-day job, and will give you additional input to how you will fit well in that culture.

4. End the interview with one of the following questions. The best way to leave an interview is to energetically let the interviewer know you want the position and there is nothing wrong with being direct about that.

After talking with you, I think I'm a good fit for this company. If I don't get the position, what would have been your biggest concern?

This will give you a chance to open a dialogue about any concerns or misconceptions the interviewer might have had about you.

Or

After talking with you, I think I'm a good fit for this company. I'm really looking forward to getting the call to begin working here. Do you think I have a good chance to get the opportunity?

This will have the same effect as the first question, opening the conversation to explain issues that you might have otherwise not had the chance to clear up.

Some other questions you might think about asking include these:

5. What excites you about coming to work? Questions like this will help form a bond with the interviewer, because you are asking about them.

6. If I am hired, what could I do to exceed expectations? This shows you are already planning for success with the company.

7. What is the best way my position can help the company toward its goals? Same idea as above shows you are already planning how to add the most value in your position to help the company.

Biggest Mistakes during an Interview

Hiring managers have discussed some of the biggest mistakes people can make during the interview.

1. Not dressed well; clothes that do not fit or are wrinkled or they looked disheveled or unclean. If you cannot dress for the interview, how are you going to dress for work every day? You have to show that you care.

Remember what I said before. If you are close in line for the position, the way you are dressed could be the deciding factor.

2. No smiling. If you are not personable, who is going to want to hire you and work with you every day?

3. Lack of eye contact during the interview. This shows nervousness and that you could be hiding things. You must have eye contact to make a personal bond.

4. Bad posture, fidgeting, and a weak handshake. None of these display an attitude of confidence and enthusiasm.

5. Crossing your arms in front of you will make you seem closed off and not open to conversations or ideas.

6. Speaking in a weak voice and using poor vocabulary and grammar.

7. Do not make the interview all about you.

8. Don't over explain why you lost your last job, and don't make it seem like you are not over your last job.

9. Do not wing the interview. Not only is it disrespectful, but it is wasting your time; you will not get the job. Here are a few tips on body language to help you in the interview.

1. If you arrive wearing outerwear, hang it up, leave it in the waiting room, or give it to the receptionist. When you get called in by the

interviewer, you want as little in your hands as possible, otherwise you can look sloppy and unorganized. Also, when you arrive, the receptionist will probably ask you to have a seat. Remain standing with your hands clasped behind your back, rocking slowly back and forth on your feet. This is a sign you are calm and collected while you wait.

2. When you are told to enter the interviewer's office, walk through the door and maintain the same pace. Nervous people will hesitate or change their speed as they move through the doorway.

3. When you walk in, do so at a medium pace. When you get to your place in the room, put down whatever is in your hands, shake hands (only if the interviewer first offers to do so), and sit down. This will show you aren't use to being kept waiting and you are comfortable walking into people's offices.

4. If you shake the other person's hand, do not shake directly over the desk—step to the side. Try to use the person's name at least twice in the first 15 seconds.

5. Mirror the interviewer's body language, when appropriate, to build a subconscious bond between the two of you.

6. When you leave the room, repack your things in a controlled manner, do not rush in a frenzy. Shake hands and thank the interviewer for his or her time. When you leave, people will watch and inspect you. Men, you need to shine the back of your shoes, as this is what is noticed the most as you leave the room. Women, studies show that interviewers look at your buttocks as you leave. So, when you get to the door, turn around and smile, so they remember you, not your buttocks.

7. Bonus advice! If you don't know what to do with your hands during the interview, just limit hand gestures. People who feel important use fewer hand gestures than people who do not.

After the Interview

Follow up with an email to say thank you for the interviewer's time. Also mail a handwritten thank-you note. You have to be professional. Even if the company doesn't hire you, if you came in second and you are polite and follow-up, the interviewer might pass your name to someone they know.

Realize that not all interviews will go well. Learn from any mistakes you made and any parts of the interview that you felt you were underprepared for. There are also some interviewers you just won't have chemistry with. Whether it is because of previous bias or one of you just showed up in a bad mood. The point is they also might have already interviewed someone they like for the position, and they didn't want to cancel on you at the last minute. Drive on and crush the next interview.

9 Entrepreneurship

"If opportunity doesn't knock, build a door."
—Milton Berle

So You Want to Be an Entrepreneur

Many people leaving the military have the skills to be their own boss. There are many successful small businesses that are thriving. Here is one thing I want to tell you. It takes more work than you might think. You are the boss, and you are the one deciding whether you succeed or not. A lot of entrepreneurs have been on the verge of bankruptcy before their businesses began to flourish. That being said, if you're still interested, let's get into the details.

Why Do You Want to Be an Entrepreneur

You have to decide why you want to be an entrepreneur. Like I said, it isn't for everyone. There are many reasons why people want to start their own businesses. Most of the time people want to change their circumstances.

Here is the deal. It is easier for a single, young person to take a chance and begin a business. However, a married person with kids and a mortgage can still do it, but it will be harder and much more stressful. The only thing you need is an idea for which people want to give you money and the grit, determination, and energy to work countless hours a day and get the work done.

Identify Your Business

What kind of service or product do you want to sell? Having an idea is just the beginning. You need to conduct your market research to make sure people want to give you money for your idea. Are there other products or services like yours? If there isn't anything like what you are planning to do, chances are there is a reason for that. No one wants it.

Here are some steps to take to make sure you are identifying a viable business. What do you know how to do? Is there a skill or ability you have that you can market without a learning curve? If there is, you can start doing your research to see if people want that.

Check out what other people are doing. What are other businesses in your area doing that you can put your individual twist on? Make sure the market isn't oversaturated. Do your best to emulate it.

The other way to decide your business is to solve a common problem. Think of something you, or the people you know, would buy without thinking about it if you saw it for sale. That is how you find the perfect product. You would know how to market it and you would know your target audience. The downside is that this comes with the most risk.

This Is Not a Hobby

You are working to start a business, and you have to keep that in mind. Your mindset can determine your success. If you are not ready to be serious about the endeavor you are going into, you are better off working for someone besides yourself. You have to have complete confidence in yourself and your business. There will be enough people doubting you, if you are one of them, you have a greater chance of failure.

Part of your business is planning, especially in the infancy stages of the business. You are going to have to plan everything, and the easiest way to do this is by creating an in-depth business plan. I have templates from the small business administration on my website (crushyourtransition.com) for you to download and use. They are self-explanatory. The business plan also functions as a timeline for your goals and how you plan to achieve them. The process is similar to the one you used earlier with your individual transition plan to map out your goals and milestones.

It's Not about You

When you are beginning a new business, you need to remember one thing. Your business is not about you. Your customers will make or break you. **First**, without having a large customer base, you will rely on customers to spread the word about your business to bring in new customers. **Second**, you want to turn your new customers into repeat customers. **Third**, you need to have good customer service and all of your policies and procedures have to be geared toward making the customers happy.

Along with maintaining good relationships with your customers, you have to follow up with them. This will give you personal interaction with them to help make them feel special, and they will know you really care about them. The opportunity to talk to the customers gives you the chance to see what they like about your business and what else you might want to offer them. You have to constantly be searching for any gaps that might hurt your customers' views of your business.

Don't Try to Be a Hero

One major shortfall that new entrepreneurs face is trying to take on too much themselves. People have a hard time outsourcing specific areas of work that need to be done. If you attempt to do everything, you will either end up taking shortcuts to get things accomplished or you will sacrifice quality on your product. When I began writing this book, my intent was to try to do everything myself, including the cover and the editing. I quickly realized that if I tried to do everything without hiring a team of people to assist me, my product would suffer due to my stubbornness.

I ended up hiring a freelance graphic designer and an editor, which did two things for me. First, my finished product was professional and well done. Also the project was finished at least a month faster by having a team. I had the cover designed as I finished writing the book, and I was able to begin promoting the book as it was being edited. Although it was more expensive, I was able to get a better product to the customer in less time.

The Military Advantage

Why do I say that military people have an advantage? If you are smart and preparing two to three years before exiting the service, you have the ability to test your business plan without a lot of the normal risks involved.

There is no need to go into a business immediately, working to make a million dollars. You can be a "sidepreneur" and begin a part-time venture while you are still serving. Start your business early and you can work out some of the kinks, slowly get over the learning curve, and make a little extra money.

If you can get started on a smaller level while you still have a steady paycheck, you can really work out the issues in your business. If you can make an extra $500 a month that you can save for growing your business, use it to reduce your debt before leaving the service, and use those acquired business skills on your résumé if you later decide that taking your business fulltime isn't for you.

10 Fear

"Ultimately we know deeply that the other side of every fear is freedom."
—Marilyn Ferguson

Facing Your Fear

I have a secret for you. We are all afraid. We have been throughout our lives. You just have to get past it. I've been afraid every page of this book. Yes, it is hard for me to admit that. However, it is hard to put your thoughts out there and know you will be judged by your words. The point is, I didn't let that stop me. Every small step you take builds more courage, and over time you will take larger steps until you arrive at your goal.

If I can do it, so can you. There are a couple of ways to do this, but I have the resources to get you on the road to freedom. Your attitude can be your best weapon against fear. You have to believe that you can do anything you put your mind to. One way to do this is to journal your successes, and, when you begin to doubt yourself, look back at those successes to inspire you to continue.

Many times it's not just you holding you back. Have you ever had someone you know, a close friend or family member, who told you that you are just being crazy and you need to stop dreaming? They truly were not that worried about what you were doing. They were thinking about their fears and what they would do in your situation. You have to live your life and sometimes your gut knows what is best for you. There were many people close to me who I didn't tell about this book, because I didn't want to hear what they had to say. I waited until I was almost finished and then they could only support me, because I was almost at the end of the race.

You are at a pivotal time in your life. Are you going to go into this next phase playing it safe, or are you going to take a chance? Think about three things you are afraid of in regard to your career transition. Write them down. Now think about two ways you can work to reduce those fears.

Once you identify what your fears are, you can begin to move past them. Think of your fears as the little devil on your shoulder telling you what you can't do. He might say, "You're not qualified" or "Why do you think you are able to do that?" Think for a minute about what your devil tells you to discourage you from trying to achieve your goals when you examine what you want to do.

Now that you are making the connection to what you are telling yourself to hold you back, you can look deeper. What effect is it having on you? Is it keeping you from advancing in your career field or switching to a career field you want to be a part of? You need to know these things and keep looking at yourself. You need to understand your self-imposed fears before you can begin to get past them.

It's easy for people to tell you not to be afraid. However, the truth is sometimes it's easier to be in a gunfight than face our own fears. Think of what you can do to get past your devil. Learn to manage your fear, talk back to it. That is what I use. I have internal agreements with my devil all the time. His name is Dan. I encourage you to also name your devil. It is easier to argue with someone who has a name.

Until you learn to get past those fears, you will not find happiness and a life of freedom. You will continue to feel unfulfilled. Ask yourself, would you rather try and fail or just fail to try? If you have read this far into the book, I don't think you are going with the latter.

Email me and I'll help you, if your fear is the only thing holding you back from success.

11 Success

Facing Your Success

We've covered a lot of topics in these pages. My hope is that you will see your success as a veteran in the military as a steppingstone to your success in a civilian career. I have helped to guide you through the process so you can *Crush Your Military Transition.*

You are now one of the people who knows and understands the best way to build your confidence to make your transition successful. Through this book, I have offered suggestions, ideas, and exercises that will help you discover what careers you are best suited for and help you find a new occupation. It's exciting to move forward to the next phase of your life.

Remember that you are not alone. As a veteran, you are surrounded by many others who have been where you are. They translated their military skills to civilian skills and readjusted to have successful civilian lives. You can too!

You will be successful. You are ready to face this challenge, just as you have other challenges throughout your life. You are prepared to trade in your military uniform for civilian clothes. You have the tools to get started doing what you truly want to do—live how you want to live.

Are you ready to define your new life and begin to control your own destiny? I hope you answer with a resounding "YES!"

About the Author

Jeffrey Phillipy is devoted to helping people improve their lives. His passion in life is mentoring leaders to teach them to reach their full potential.

Links to Social Media

LinkedIn
LinkedIn.com/jeffreyphillipy

Facebook
Facebook.com/jeffrey.phillipy

Twitter
Twitter.com/Jeffreyphillipy

Website
crushyourtransition.com & jphillipy.com

Email
jeff@crushyourtransition.com

www.ingramcontent.com/pod-product-compliance
Lightning Source LLC
Chambersburg PA
CBHW081256040426
42452CB00014B/2527